Arizona Family Field Trips

By Marty Campbell

Published by
Marty Campbell
3116 E. Escuda Rd.
Phoenix, AZ 85050

Cover Design by Ken Jackway, Amigos de Arizonac, Inc.

©Copyright 1999 by Marty Campbell
Second edition 2002

Printed in the U.S.A

ISBN 0-9722286-0-8

Dedication

This book is dedicated to my wife, Patty, whose patience, forgiveness and faith in me knows no bounds. I can't imagine a road trip without her.

A Word About Maps and Destination Access

Please note that the maps included in this book are for general reference and are not to scale. Please consult a reputable highway or topo map for specific locations and distances.

Rural roadways in Arizona can twist and turn, particularly in the mountains. A good map is an essential tool for anyone traveling roadways or hiking trails.

Things change! Natural occurances and human decisions may affect destination access. Please check destination access prior to departing on an Arizona adventure.

Precautions

Physical hazards may be encountered when visiting the areas described in this book. Readers should take proper precautions, take account of their physical fitness and make local inquiries, as author and publisher cannot accept responsibility for such matters.

- Vehicles must be in good condition, with emphasis on: tires (including spare), brakes, hoses & belts, coolant, oil.
- Gas, food, water and first aid supplies must be sufficient for trip.
- Always have a minimum of 1 gallon of water for everyone; more is better.
- Leave a written itinerary with a responsible person. Include: destination, route, expected return time and vehicle description. Do not change your itinerary. Instruct person to contact authorities if you are more than one hour overdue.
- If you break down, stay with your vehicle.

To order my comprehensive *Arizona Outdoor Survival and Safety Guide*, enclose $4.95 (includes shipping & handling), and mail to: Marty Cambell, 3116 E. Escuda Road, Phoenix, AZ 85050. Make checks payable to Marty Campbell.

— *Marty Campbell*

Foreword

He had me in the first paragraph.

Writing about a family train trip through Verde Canyon, Marty Campbell described a pair of bald eagles plunging from red sandstone cliffs, "accelerating like lethal missiles" until they met air currents rising from the canyon floor.

It was the first "Arizona Family Field Trips" column that Marty wrote for *Raising Arizona Kids Magazine* and I — like thousands of other Valley parents — was captivated by his vivid descriptions of an Arizona that I had yet to experience or share with my children.

That was eight years ago. Marty's column has become such a popular staple in the magazine (it's consistently ranked first among our editorial departments in reader surveys) that I can't imagine a time when his adventures weren't part of it. Marty has taken us — along with his wife Patty and daughters Merritt and Alexis — digging for ancient pottery and hiking past splendid displays of hieroglyphics. He's guided us through magnificent canyons and into lonely, eerie ghost towns. He's taken us fly fishing and kayaking and pontoon boating. He's taught us Arizona history lessons both profound and quirky and he's shown us how much fun our great state can be.

To parents burdened — by choice, certainly, but no less wistfully — to the responsibility and periodic drudgery of home, hearth, hectic schedules and Happy Meals, Marty's writing always has carried a hopeful message: If he can "get away from it all" — and take his kids, no less — so can we.

In this newest project, *Arizona Family Field Trips*, the book, Marty makes following that dream as easy as following a recipe. And, speaking as someone whose family has enjoyed many of his field trips during the past four years, I can't wait to hit the road.

Karen Barr
Editor & Publisher
Raising Arizona Kids Magazine

Preface

Grandma Marie's '61 Chevy Belair was overheating, and I was really steamed. "How in the name of Sam Hill," I asked myself for the umpteenth time, "could my otherwise intelligent, understanding parents pull up stakes in Montana and re-locate to this worthless inferno?"

It was August 18th, 1968. The thermometer on the old, blue Biddulph Auto sign on the west side of I-17 flashed 118 degrees. It was at least that in the Belair that wasn't equipped with air conditioning. As the old beater limped into Phoenix, I vowed that when I graduated from high school, I'd buy my own set of wheels, and the last I'd see of Arizona would be in the rear view mirror.

The following spring, the late Arizona Senator and 1964 presidential candidate, Barry M. Goldwater, delivered the keynote address at my high school commencement. It was the height of the Vietnam War, and many in the young, hostile audience were less than enthusiastic about the Senator's fiery remarks regarding patriotism and commitment. I include myself. Still, the speech was one of the finest I have ever heard, and I had to hand it to Senator Goldwater for his straight-shooting rhetoric. Listening intently, I remembered a portion of another Goldwater speech that I read in my Arizona History textbook. Speaking at the Heard Museum, Goldwater threw down the gauntlet.

"I don't care how long you live in this state, you never get tired of it. And, you never really see it all," he said. "If you have a car, get out and see this state."

I took the challenge.

Shortly after receiving my diploma, I did purchase my own car, a brand new Ford Maverick, putting myself in debt to the tune of $1,995. Before demolishing the car in a freeway accident, I racked up thousands of miles on exciting adventures, never once leaving Arizona. You guessed it. I have never returned to Montana. Barry Goldwater was right. You really can't see all of Arizona, but I'm still trying.

My road trip companions are my beautiful wife, Patty, and our daughters, Merritt and Alexis. Together, we travel the highways and byways of Arizona, and seldom take an out-of-state vacation. Many of our discoveries are featured each month in my column, Arizona Family Field Trips, that I write for *Raising Arizona Kids* magazine. In fact, the idea for this book came about, in part, as a result of inquires and comments from readers.

It is my hope that this guide will jump-start or enhance your sense of adventure when you're on the Arizona roads. I never intended for this book to be read once, and stashed away on a shelf. It has been designed to fit neatly in a console or door pouch of your vehicle. You can flatten it out or fold it in half. Hey, it's a travel guide, not an expensive coffee table showpiece. When you head down the road, put it to good work. Find some places along your route and pay a visit. There's a pretty fair chance we'll run into one another.

Good exploring, and be safe.

Acknowledgments

Authors have the satisfaction of seeing their name on the cover of book. Most books, however, are the result of a team effort, and this book is no exception. I'm indebted to the following people who helped make this book a reality:

- Karen Barr, Editor and Publisher of *Raising Arizona Kids* magazine, who gambled on a story idea that evolved into my monthly column, Arizona Family Field Trips. That vote of confidence got the ball rolling. Karen has also been an advisor and very special friend.
- Ken Jackway of Amigos de Arizonac, Inc. for his creativity, advice, and friendship.
- The wonderful individuals who believed enough in this project to help with finances.
- The staff at *Raising Arizona Kids* magazine for their encouragement and friendship.

Table of Contents

Chapter One: Southern Arizona

Chapter Two: Central Mountains & Mogollon Rim

Chapter Three: Central Arizona

Chapter Seven: Western Arizona

Chapter Eight: East-Central Arizona and White Mountains

Chapter Nine: North-Central Arizona

Arizona's Newest National Monuments

Southern Arizona Map

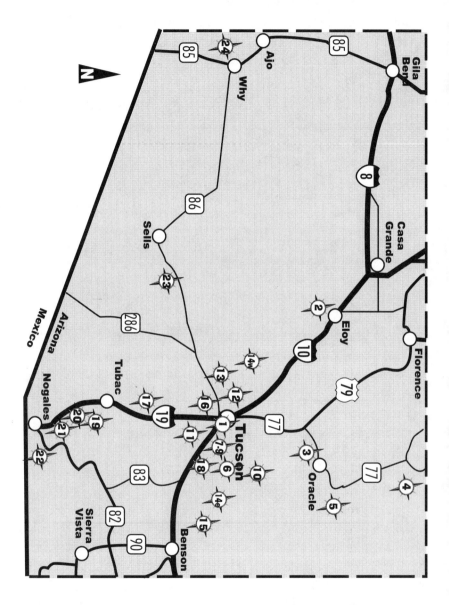

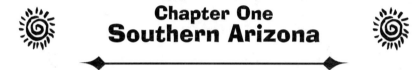

Chapter One
Southern Arizona

In the late 1600s, Father Eusebio Francisco Kino, already a middle-aged Jesuit missionary, entered the rugged territory that is present-day southern Arizona. The revered (and candidate for sainthood) "Padre on Horseback" turned mud into churches and river deltas into farms.

Padre Kino's heroic achievements in a land called Pimeria Alta (Upper Pima Land) led to further exploration and settlement. Centuries of history, enriched by the wonderful cultures of the Spanish, Mexicans, Native Americans and Europeans enhances an explore of this fascinating region of Arizona.

Tucson is Arizona's second largest city and the starting point for discovering southern Arizona. Like Phoenix, Tucson is experiencing incredible growth. Still, *The Old Pueblo* retains the charm of a small community.

In and around Tucson you'll find fascinating museums, a national park that's divided in two, a sealed ecosystem, terrific hiking trails and a White Dove.

South of Tucson, descend into the largest dry cave in the world and shiver when you explore the doomsday cavern. With a park ranger as your guide, hike to a "Kino Mission" that only a few lucky people have seen. If fishing, swimming and camping are in your plans, Patagonia Lake State Park is worth a try. The artist community of Tubac, the site of the first European settlement in Arizona, is only 15 miles from the Mexican border. Nogales is Arizona's largest border community, offering unique shopping and excellent Sonoran-style dining. From the border, we'll take a 53-mile drive on a dirt road and discover a desert oasis surrounded by organ pipe cacti. On the final leg of our journey through southern Arizona, we'll drive to the top of a mountain and stargaze at galaxies far, far away.

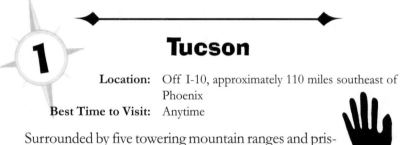

Tucson

Location:	Off I-10, approximately 110 miles southeast of Phoenix
Best Time to Visit:	Anytime

Surrounded by five towering mountain ranges and pristine Sonoran Desert, Tucson is a big city with a small town feel and look. Business and tourism are booming in the *Old Pueblo*. The University of Arizona, located near the financial district, is internationally renowned for its top-notch medical and law schools.

In a limited space, I can only list a handful of my family's favorite places in and near Tucson. When planning a visit to Tucson, contact the Metropolitan Tucson Convention and Visitors Bureau and they will provided detailed information about this charming city.

Metropolitan Tucson Convention & Visitors Bureau, 130 S. Scott Ave., Tucson, AZ 85701, 520-624-1817 or 800-638-8350

2 Picacho Peak State Park

Location:	Off I-10, 40 miles north of Tucson
Best Time to Visit:	Spring, fall, winter
Visitor Center/Museum:	Yes
Hours:	Visitor center 8 a.m.- 5 p.m. daily, except Christmas; campground 24 hrs.
Fee Area:	Yes; day use $6 per vehicle; tent camping $12 per vehicle; electrical hook-ups $17 per vehicle
Restroom:	Yes; barrier-free
Wheelchair/Stroller Access:	Yes; at visitor center; limited on grounds
Drinking Water:	Yes
Picnic Area:	Yes
Lodging:	No
Camping:	Yes
Suitable for:	All ages

Picacho Peak State Park, located about 40-miles north of Tucson, is a prominent landmark. Like several other sites in Arizona, the name is redundant. Picacho is Spanish for peak. So we have Peak Peak.

On this site a small Civil War skirmish was fought, resulting in the death of three Union soldiers. A re-enactment of that fight, and several other southwestern battles, takes place during Archaeology Awareness Month, usually in March.

Picacho Peak State Park offers excellent hiking opportunities, ranging from easy to very difficult. It is also a popular camping destination.

Picacho Peak State Park, P.O. Box 275, Picacho, AZ 85241, 520-466-3183

3 **Oracle State Park**

Location:	Off Old Mt. Lemmon Rd., just past the town of Oracle from Hwy. 77 north
Best Time to Visit:	Spring, fall, winter
Visitor Center/Museum:	Yes
Hours:	8 a.m.- 5 p.m. daily, except Christmas; day use park only
Fee Area:	Yes; $5 per vehicle up to four passengers; $1 per person for additional occupants. School year Nature Education Programs: $1 per student
Restroom:	Yes; barrier-free
Wheelchair/Stroller Access:	Yes; in most areas
Drinking Water:	Yes
Picnic Area:	Yes; some with ramadas
Lodging:	No
Camping:	No
Suitable for:	All ages

Located in the northeastern foothills of the Santa Catalina Mountains, Oracle State Park is a nearly 4,000-acre preserve consisting of oak grassland, riparian woodland, and mesquite scrub habitats that support a diversity of wildlife. The park serves as an environmental education center and a wildlife refuge.

Nature education programs, geared for all ages, are offered to school students at a very reasonable fee.

Bird watching, picnicking and hiking, (including a seven mile section of the border-to-border Arizona Trail) are all popular activities at this new park..

Oracle State Park, P.O. Box 700, Oracle, AZ 85623, 520-896-2425

4   Biosphere 2

Location:	Off AZ 77 @ mile marker 96.5 near Oracle; 35-40 minutes north of Tucson
Best Time to Visit:	Anytime
Visitor Center/Museum:	Yes; with gift shops
Hours:	Daily 9 a.m.-5 p.m., except major holidays; guided tours hourly 9 a.m.-4 p.m.
Fee Area:	Yes; adults $12.95; seniors $10.95; 6-17 $6; under 6 free
Restroom:	Yes; barrier-free
Wheelchair/Stroller Access:	Yes; all exhibits and presentations. Wheelchairs & strollers available for rent
Drinking Water:	Yes
Picnic Area:	No; picnicking & pets prohibited
Lodging:	Yes; hotel suites; rates vary with season, but are reasonable
Camping:	No
Suitable for:	All ages
Notes/Tips:	Unique educational programs available for school groups K-12. Canyon Cafe offers complete meals/beverages; Bio 2 Cyber Cafe is a computer/coffee shop

The original Biosphere, a sealed, self-contained habitation project, was mired in controversy. As a scientific experiment, Biosphere was a fiasco and even became a running joke on late night TV talk shows.

In 1995, the new Biosphere 2 and Columbia University teamed-up, turned the operation profitable, and created a fascinating educational facility.

Within the huge enclosures you'll discover an ocean, tropical rain forest, marsh, desert, savanna and scrub land. The guided walking tours, that last about 90 minutes, don't actually enter the plexiglass domes. You look inside through observation windows.

Biosphere 2, P.O. Box 689, Oracle, AZ 85623, 800-828-2462, Fax: 520-896-6429

5 Catalina State Park

Location:	About half-way between Oracle & Tucson off AZ 77
Best Time to Visit:	Spring, fall, winter
Visitor Center/Museum:	Yes
Hours:	24 hrs., 7 days a week
Fee Area:	Yes; day use $6; primitive/tent camping $12; electrical hook-ups $17
Restroom:	Yes; not barrier-free
Wheelchair/Stroller Access:	Limited; portions of some hiking trails will accommodate chairs/strollers
Drinking Water:	Yes
Picnic Area:	Yes
Lodging:	No
Camping:	Yes; electric hook-ups & dump station
Suitable for:	All ages
Notes/Tips:	When visiting, take the stunning 28-mile drive to the top of Mt. Lemmon, the southern-most ski area in the United States. The scenery is spectacular. Before taking the drive, contact the Coronado National Forest @ 520-749-8700 for road conditions or restrictions.

Located at the base of Mt. Lemmon in the beautiful Santa Catalina Mountains, Catalina State Park has something for everyone, from camping under desert skies, to hiking through canyons and streams, to picnicking and bird watching. An equestrian area is also available.

Catalina State Park, P.O. Box 36986, Tucson, AZ 85740, 520-628-5798

6 Mt. Lemmon/ Catalina Scenic Highway

Location:	25 miles from downtown Tucson on the Catalina Scenic Highway
Best Time to Visit:	Anytime; but please see notes/tips below
Visitor Center/Museum:	Yes; in Ski Valley & Summerhaven
Hours:	The drive up Mt. Lemmon on the Catalina highway can be taken at anytime. Snow skiing is seasonal.
Fee Area:	Yes and no: Driving *non-stop* to and from Summerhaven does not require a fee. To park anywhere along the highway, however; requires purchasing a $5 day pass. Week long and annual passes are $10 and $20 respectively. There are additional charges for snow skiing and summer sky rides.
Restroom:	Yes; along the highway, at picnic areas, and in Summerhaven
Wheelchair/Stroller Access:	Yes; but limited in some areas
Drinking Water:	Yes
Lodging:	Yes; hotels, motels, charming lodges, and private cabins
Camping:	Yes
Suitable for:	All ages
Notes/Tips:	Catalina Scenic Highway is a narrow mountain road that snakes up the mountain. **Drive slowly.** Heavy snowfall is common during the winter. Check road conditions before departure regarding possible closure, and/or chain requirements. Be prepared for severe winter driving conditions. **There is no gas available on the mountain—fill up before leaving Tucson.** Even in the summer, prepare for cooler, wet conditions. Summer thunderstorms on the mountain are common and powerful. Temperature can drop dramatically. Seek shelter if lightning begins.

Twenty-five miles and 9,000 feet about Tucson's desert floor you'll find a completely different world. The beautiful drive up the twisting Catalina Highway takes you through four distinct ecological zones, from stately saguaro cactus at the bottom, to pine and aspen groves at the top.

Outdoor activities in the summer include hiking, rock climbing, picnicking, camping, fishing, and exciting sky rides on the chairlifts at Ski Valley. Dining, browsing, and shopping are all available in the alpine community of Summerhaven. In the winter, go skiing and sledding at Ski Valley, the nation's southern most ski resort.

Mt. Lemmon/Summerhaven information, www.mt-lemmon.com, e-mail at Webmaster@mtlemmon.com

Arizona State Museum

7

Location:	In central Tucson, on the University of Arizona Campus
Best Time to Visit:	Anytime
Visitor Center/Museum:	Yes
Hours:	Mon.-Sat. 10 a.m.-5 p.m.; Sun. noon-5 p.m. Closed major holidays
Fee Area:	No; donations accepted
Restroom:	Yes; barrier-free
Wheelchair/Stroller Access:	Yes; entire facility
Drinking Water:	Yes
Picnic Area:	No
Lodging:	No; in Tucson, of course
Camping:	No
Suitable for:	All ages

Built when the west was really wild (the original structure dates to 1893) The Arizona State Museum is the oldest and one of the finest museums in the state.

Located on the University of Arizona campus, the many exhibits include fascinating fossil displays and artifacts from Arizona's prehistory. "Paths of Life: American Indians of the Southwest" is a fascinating exhibit and occupies 10,000 sq. ft. Video presentations and displays highlight the contemporary lives of native peoples of Arizona and our neighbors to the south in Sonora, Mexico.

Arizona State Museum, 1013 East University, Tucson, AZ 85721, 520-621-6302

Flandrau Science Center

8

Location:	At the corner of Cherry Avenue and University on the U of A campus
Best Time to Visit:	Anytime
Visitor Center/Museum:	Yes
Hours:	Mon.-Sat. 9 a.m.-5 p.m.; Wed.-Sat. 7 p.m.-9 p.m.; Sun. 1 p.m.-5 p.m.
Fee Area:	Yes; Exhibit admission: $3 adults; $2 children; free for children under 3. Planetarium admission: $5 adults; $4.50 seniors (55+), U of A staff, military; $4 children. Specials: $7 double feature; $9 triple feature
Restroom:	Yes; barrier-free
Wheelchair/Stroller Access:	Yes
Drinking Water:	Yes
Picnic Area:	No
Lodging:	No; in Tucson
Camping:	No
Suitable for:	All ages
Notes/Tips:	Children under 3 are not admitted to planetarium. Allow at least a half-day to really experience this exciting science center.

Discovery is what the Flandrau Science Center is all about. There is so much to see and do at this renowned center, you'll want to visit more than once. From astronomy to rocks and minerals, this science center has it all. But this is no stuffy, hands-off museum. In fact, hands-on education is the order of the day. Whatever you do, don't skip the Planetarium experience. This monstrous multimedia theater will take you on a tour of the universe employing 30 projectors, two high-tech video systems, and a killer sound system.

Flandrau Science Center, 1601 East University Blvd., Tucson, AZ 85719, 520-621-7827

---

9 Arizona Historical Society's Museum

Location:	On the University of Arizona campus @ 2nd & Euclid streets
Best Time to Visit:	Anytime
Visitor Center/Museum:	Yes
Hours:	Mon.-Sat. 10 a.m.- 4 p.m.; Sun. noon - 4 p.m.; excluding holidays
Fee Area:	Yes; 13 & up $8.95; 6-12 $1.75; under 6 free
Restroom:	Yes; barrier-free
Wheelchair/Stroller Access:	Yes; wheelchairs & strollers available for free
Drinking Water:	Yes
Picnic Area:	No
Lodging:	No; in Tucson
Camping:	No
Suitable for:	All ages

Also situated on the U of A campus, this marvelous museum features exhibits that focus on Arizona's pre-history and cultures, Spanish colonialization and influence, territorial and mining days and recent history after statehood.

The library collection is outstanding and includes a fascinating display of historical photographs.

Arizona Historical Society's Museum, 949 E. 2nd St., Tucson, AZ 85743, 520-628-5774

Sabino Canyon

10

Location:	In northeast Tucson off Sabino Canyon Rd. in Catalina foothills area
Best Time to Visit:	Anytime
Visitor Center/Museum:	Yes
Hours:	Weekdays 8 a.m - 4:30 p.m.; weekends 8:30 a.m.- 4:30 p.m.; Closed Christmas Day
Fee Area:	Tram - adults $6; 3-12 $2.50; under 3 free. Bear Canyon tram - all passengers $3
Restroom:	Yes; at visitor center
Wheelchair/Stroller Access:	Yes; but call in advance to reserve spaces on the tram
Drinking Water:	Yes
Picnic Area:	Yes
Lodging:	No
Camping:	No
Suitable for:	All ages
Notes/Tips:	The Bear Canyon hike to Seven Falls is rated as moderately difficult and not suitable for small children. All hikers are required to have a minimum of a quart of water. I suggest more.

One of the most popular hiking and picnicking spots in Tucson, Sabino Canyon features several streams with clear, cool swimming holes, waterfalls and beautiful scenery.

Cars are not permitted in the canyon. However, a tram takes visitors to the top of the gorge. Passengers can jump on-and-off the tram at nine different stops. Wonderful night-time tram rides are available with reservations.

A different tram takes hikers to nearby Bear Canyon and the trailhead that leads to spectacular Seven Falls.

Sabino Canyon, 5700 N. Sabino Canyon Rd., Tucson, AZ 85750, 520-749-8700 (visitor center) or 520-749-2861 (recorded tram info)

Tohono Chul Park

Location:	On Paseo del Norte approximately five miles east of the intersection of I-10 and Ina Road
Best Time to Visit:	Spring, fall, winter
Visitor Center/Museum:	Yes
Hours:	Park grounds: 7 a.m.-sunset daily; Galleries & Museum Shops: 9:30 a.m.-5 p.m. Mon.-Sat & 11 a.m.-5 p.m. Sun.; Plant Interpretation Center & Greenhouse: 9 a.m.-12 p.m. June through Labor Day & 10 a.m.-4 p.m. the remainder of the year; Tea Room: 8 a.m.-5 p.m. daily
Fee Area:	No; but a $2 donation is encouraged and appreciated
Restroom:	Yes; barrier free
Wheelchair/Stroller Access:	Yes; none of the discovery trails are paved, but most are accessible. Those that are not are clearly marked. All buildings are accessible. A wheelchair is available in the Exhibit Hall.
Drinking Water:	Yes
Picnic Area:	Just a patio at the Tea Room
Lodging:	No
Camping:	No
Suitable for:	All ages

Tohono Chul Park is the Southwest's center where nature, art, and culture connect. You can walk down the nature trails through the center's splendid gardens, tour the Exhibit Hall in a renovated historic home, enjoy breakfast, lunch or afternoon tea in the Tea Room.

This peaceful park is truly a place of beauty where you'll experience the wonders of the Sonoran Desert, and gain knowledge of the natural and cultural heritage of the region.

Tohono Chul Park, 7366 N. Paseo del Norte, Tucson, AZ 85704, 520-742-6455

Old Tucson Studios

12

Location:	Off South Kinney Rd., 12 miles west of Tucson. Call for directions
Best Time to Visit:	Spring, fall, winter
Visitor Center/Museum:	Yes
Hours:	Late Dec.- mid-Apr. 9 a.m.- 7 p.m.; rest of year 10 a.m.- 6 p.m. Closed Thanksgiving & Christmas
Fee Area:	Yes; adult $14.95; ages 4 -11 $9.45; under 4 free. Prices reduced for residents of Pima County
Restroom:	Yes; barrier-free
Wheelchair/Stroller Access:	Yes; entire complex. However, as a western town, the streets are comprised of sand and dirt. Wheelchairs available at no charge
Drinking Water:	Yes
Picnic Area:	Yes; with shaded tables
Lodging:	No
Camping:	No
Suitable for:	All ages
Notes/Tips:	Parking is free. Handicapped & RV parking available. Leashed pets are welcome. Families may carry in picnic baskets (excluding alcoholic beverages). There are three restaurants, a cantina, an ice-cream parlor and a sweet shop.

Old Tucson Studios is a western theme park and motion picture studio located 12 miles west of Tucson.

The studio came to life in 1939 when Columbia Pictures built a replica of 1860s Tucson for the film *Arizona*. The studio was used in the filming of *The Bells of St. Mary's*, starring Bing Crosby and Ingrid Bergman; *Winchester 73* with Jimmy Stewart; and the classic, *Gunfight at the OK Corral* starring Burt Lancaster and Kirk Douglas. John Wayne filmed four movies here. Dozens of television programs were shot on the elaborate sets, with Old Tucson Studios earning the title "Hollywood in the Desert."

The huge complex is also a charming family theme park that features a mining town, an old-fashioned carnival, Town Square and a Mexican Mission Plaza.

In 1995, a devastating fire destroyed over 40 percent of the facility. After two years of re-building, the park re-opened in 1997, and is more impressive than ever.

Old Tucson Studios, 201 South Kinney Rd, Tucson, AZ 85735, 520-883-0100, Fax: 520-578-1269

13 **Arizona-Sonora Desert Museum**

Location:	Northwest of Tucson, off North Kinney Rd
Best Time to Visit:	Spring, fall, winter
Visitor Center/Museum:	Yes
Hours:	Mar.-Sept. daily 7:30 a.m.- 6 p.m.; Oct.-Feb., daily 8:30 a.m.- 5 p.m.; closed all major holidays
Fee Area:	Yes; 13 & up $8.95; 6 -12 $1.75; under 6 free
Restroom:	Yes; barrier-free
Wheelchair/Stroller Access:	Yes; entire facility. Wheelchairs & strollers available at no charge
Drinking Water:	Yes
Picnic Area:	Yes
Lodging:	No
Camping:	No
Suitable for:	All ages
Notes/Tips:	There is a restaurant, coffee bar and gift shop. Pets aren't permitted.

A non-profit educational institution that was founded in 1952, The Arizona-Sonora Desert Museum is a true gem.

The sprawling facility is poorly named, simply because it is not a museum, but a wonderful zoo. Here, you can observe scores of critters that make their home in the Sonoran Desert, all going about their business in their natural habitat. A number of excellent interactive programs are designed to foster appreciation, knowledge and wise stewardship of the fragile desert.

When visiting Tucson, particularly with kids, this attraction must be on your agenda.

Arizona-Sonora Desert Museum, 2021 N. Kinney Rd., Tucson, AZ 85743, 520-883-2702

14 Saguaro National Park

Location:	West Section - about 12 miles west of I-10 on North Kinney Rd.; East Section - about 15 miles off I-10 on South Old Spanish Trail
Best Time to Visit:	Spring, fall, winter
Visitor Center/Museum:	Yes; both locations
Hours:	West Section - Park roads daily 6 a.m.- sunset; visitor center daily 8:30 a.m.- 5 p.m. East Section - Park roads daily 7 a.m.- sunset; visitor center daily 8:30 a.m.- 5 p.m. Both locations closed Christmas Day
Fee Area:	West Section-No; East Section-$4 per vehicle, $2 by bicycle or on foot
Restroom:	Yes; barrier-free
Wheelchair/Stroller Access:	Yes at West Section; limited to visitor center at East Section
Drinking Water:	Yes; see Notes/Tips
Picnic Area:	Yes
Lodging:	No
Camping:	No
Suitable for:	West Section-all ages; East Section-best for experienced hikers
Notes/Tips:	When hiking, particularly in the East Section, prepare for rugged desert conditions. If you are not familiar with the basic requirements for desert hiking, please seek the advice of park rangers before hitting the trail. It could save your life.

Oops, make that two parks. The east and west sections of Saguaro National Park are separated by about 20 miles. Combined, you'll see the largest concentration of saguaro cacti in the world.

The entrance to the west park is located on Kinney Road, just a few miles from the Arizona-Sonora Desert Museum. The eastern section is located in the Saguaro Wilderness southeast of Tucson.

Saguaro National Park West is the smaller of the two sections, but sees far more visitors. This portion of the park features an impressive visitor center, excellent video programs and wide, easy to walk nature trails that are suitable for all ages and will accommodate wheelchairs and strollers. There are longer hiking trails that lead to a collection of Hohokam petroglyphs, or rock art.

Saguaro National Park East is situated at the base of the beautiful, but very rugged Rincon Mountains.

If stunning desert and mountain hiking through five climate zones appeals to you, this the place. A paved road leads to most of the trailheads. Be certain to stop at the visitor center to obtain maps. Hikes offered at Saguaro National Park East are more suited for experienced trekkers.

Saguaro National Park West, 2700 North Kinney Rd., Tucson, AZ 85743, 520-733-5158

Saguaro National Park East, 3693 South Old Spanish Trail, Tucson, AZ 85730, 520-733-5155

15 Colossal Cave

Location:	At the intersection of South Old Spanish Trail Rd. & Colossal Cave Rd., 6 miles off I-10
Best Time to Visit:	Spring, fall, winter
Visitor Center/Museum:	Yes
Hours:	Seasonal; call in advance
Fee Area:	Yes; 13 & up $7.50; 6-12 $4; under 6 free
Restroom:	Yes
Wheelchair/Stroller Access:	No
Drinking Water:	Yes
Picnic Area:	No

Lodging:	No
Camping:	No
Suitable for:	All ages; may be too dark & confining for young kids

Southeast of Saguaro National Park East, you'll find Colossal Cave, the world's largest dry cavern. Portions of the cave have never been explored.

Guides will lead you on a discovery of the interior, pointing out and describing the fascinating geological formations. The path is easy to negotiate. However, at several spots there are drop-offs. Be sure to hold hands with young kids.

An old legend tells of a stash of money that was taken in a stage-coach robbery, hidden in the cave, and never found. But the cave itself is the real treasure.

Colossal Cave, P.O. Box 70, Vail, AZ 85641, 520-647-7275

Mission San Xavier del Bac

16

Location:	Off I-19 on San Xavier Rd., 10 miles southwest of Tucson
Best Time to Visit:	Anytime; Sunday is usually crowded
Visitor Center Museum:	Yes
Hours:	Not firm; gift shop open 8 a.m.- 6 p.m. summer; 9 a.m.- 5 p.m. winter
Fee Area:	No
Restroom:	Yes
Wheelchair/Stroller Access:	Yes
Drinking Water:	Yes
Picnic Area:	Yes; but small
Lodging:	No
Camping:	No
Suitable for:	All ages
Notes/Tips:	Speak quietly and be respectful of the people you'll see praying. Be courteous when using flash photography. Men should remove their hats.

Called "The White Dove of the Desert," Mission San Xavier del Bac is one of the most photographed locations in Arizona; justifiably so.

On or very near the site of the present church, the legendary Padre Kino built his adobe chapel, the northern most of the "Kino Missions." The facility seen today was completed by Franciscans in 1797 and is the oldest active Catholic church in the United States. It is arguably the finest example of Spanish Colonial architecture in the United States.

The facade over the arched entrance is magnificent. If you look closely, you'll see a cat on one side of the arch, a mouse on the opposite side. A popular legend says that if the cat catches the mouse, the world will end.

Viewing the interior of the mission is an overwhelming visual experience. After nearly a decade of delicate restoration, seeing the original colors and splendor of the frescos, paintings and statues is pure delight. This is one destination in southern Arizona that should be on your must see list.

Mission San Xavier del Bac, 1950 W. San Xavier Rd., Tucson, AZ 85746, 520-294-2624

17 Titan Missile Museum

Location:	South of Tucson off I-19 in Green Valley on Duval Mine Rd
Best Time to Visit:	Anytime **Visitor Center/Museum:** Yes; fascinating facility & theater
Hours:	May 1- Oct. 31, Wed.-Sun. 9 a.m.-5 p.m.; Nov. 1- Apr. 30 daily 9 a.m.-5 p.m.; last tour @ 4 p.m.; closed Thanksgiving & Christmas
Fee Area:	Yes; adults $6; seniors/military $5; 10-17 $3; under 10 free
Restroom:	Yes
Wheelchair/Stroller Access:	Yes, with some limitations. Special tours arranged for those needing assistance via elevator. Call in advance.

Drinking Water:	Yes
Picnic Area:	No
Lodging:	No
Camping:	No
Suitable for:	All ages

During the dark days of the Cold War, 54 Titan II missiles armed with nuclear warheads, were sheltered in hardened underground bunkers. Aimed at the former Soviet Union, the missiles could be launched within one minute of a fire order.

By 1987 all Titan II missiles and silos had been dismantled and destroyed except for missile 571-7 and its bunker.

At the Titan Missile Museum, guided tours take visitors deep underground to the silo command center. You'll learn how the crew of four lived, passed time and waited for an order that thankfully never came.

The highlight will be seeing a huge Titan Missile once capable of delivering a payload powerful enough to destroy 215 Hiroshimas.

Titan Missile Museum, 1580 W. Duval Mine Rd, P.O. Box 150, Green Valley, AZ 85622, 520-625-7736

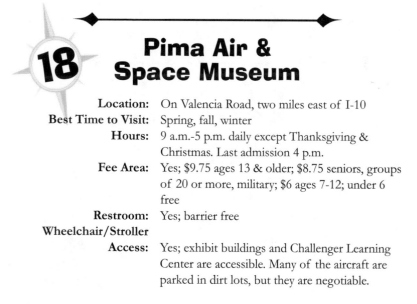

18 Pima Air & Space Museum

Location:	On Valencia Road, two miles east of I-10
Best Time to Visit:	Spring, fall, winter
Hours:	9 a.m.-5 p.m. daily except Thanksgiving & Christmas. Last admission 4 p.m.
Fee Area:	Yes; $9.75 ages 13 & older; $8.75 seniors, groups of 20 or more, military; $6 ages 7-12; under 6 free
Restroom:	Yes; barrier free
Wheelchair/Stroller Access:	Yes; exhibit buildings and Challenger Learning Center are accessible. Many of the aircraft are parked in dirt lots, but they are negotiable.

Drinking Water:	Yes
Picnic Area:	No
Lodging:	No
Camping:	No
Suitable for:	All ages
Notes/Tips:	Make reservations well in advance for the Challenger Learning Center

Aviation, from pioneer flight to space exploration is the theme of this fascinating park. Many huge buildings and hangers house vintage, historic and futuristic aircraft. Each of the unique exhibits feature hands-on activities for all ages.

Parked on 80 acres of the 150-acre museum are over 250 aircraft, including a presidential plane, World War II fighters and bombers, jet fighters and the enormous B-52 bomber. Hidden under a metal canopy, the once very top secret SR71 Blackbird spy plane resembles a craft that Star Wars creator George Lucas might have dreamed up.

A visit to the Pima Air & Space Museum would not be complete without participating in the exciting educational "space flight" at the Challenger Learning Center.

Plan on spending most of a day at this memorable museum.

Pima Air & Space Museum, 6000 East Valencia Road, Tucson, AZ 85706, 520-574-0462

19 Tubac Presidio State Historic Park

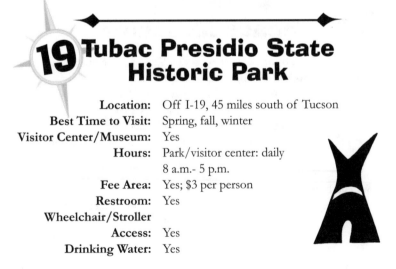

Location:	Off I-19, 45 miles south of Tucson
Best Time to Visit:	Spring, fall, winter
Visitor Center/Museum:	Yes
Hours:	Park/visitor center: daily 8 a.m.- 5 p.m.
Fee Area:	Yes; $3 per person
Restroom:	Yes
Wheelchair/Stroller Access:	Yes
Drinking Water:	Yes

Picnic Area:	Yes; shaded ramadas
Lodging:	No
Camping:	No
Suitable for:	All ages

In 1691, Padre Kino established Tubac, then a small Pima Indian village, as a mission farm and ranch. Over three decades, Spanish colonists settled here, irrigating and farming the lands along the Santa Cruz River. As the population grew, Tubac became the site of the first European town in Arizona.

Tubac Presidio is a fascinating archaeological site and charming artist community. The state park features a museum, several historic sites, a unique underground archaeology display, picnic area and living history demonstrations from October through March. Wonderful artwork and crafts are sold at 100 or so art shops.

Tubac Presidio State Historic Park, Box 1296, Tubac, AZ 85646, 520-398-2252, Fax: 520-398-2685

20 Tumacacori National Historic Park

Location:	Off I-19 @ exit 29, 3 miles south of Tubac
Best Time to Visit:	Spring, fall, winter
Visitor Center/Museum:	Yes
Hours:	8 a.m.- 5 p.m. daily; closed Thanksgiving & Christmas
Fee Area:	Yes; $2 per person (see Notes/Tips)
Restroom:	Yes; barrier-free
Wheelchair/Stroller Access:	Yes
Drinking Water:	Yes
Picnic Area:	Yes; shaded by huge trees
Lodging:	No
Camping:	No
Suitable for:	All ages
Notes/Tips:	The park has been expanded to include and preserve the ruins of Mission Guevavi and

Visita Calabazas, both built by Padre Kino. Because these are very sensitive archaeological sites, they can only be visited with a park ranger as a guide. Before visiting Tumacacori, I urge you to call in advance and make arrangements to see these two wonderful and important ruins. It will be time well spent.

• Tumacacori holds a special place in my heart. Admission is so reasonable, please put an extra dollar in the donation jar for me.

Often referred to as one of the "Kino Missions," Mission San Jose de Tumacacori was actually built by the Franciscans, long after Kino died. Padre Kino did construct a tiny chapel near the present ruins of Tumacacori, however.

The striking contrast between the magnificence of San Xavier del Bac and the adobe ruins of Tumacacori is astonishing. Before exploring the silent ruins, I spend an hour or so in the wonderful visitor center. The displays and artifacts are fascinating. A cut-away model of the church shows how the mission complex looked in the late 1700s. See Notes/Tips.

Tumacacori National Historic Park, P.O. Box 67, Tumacacori, AZ 85640, 520-398-2341

◆———————————————◆

Patagonia Lake State Park

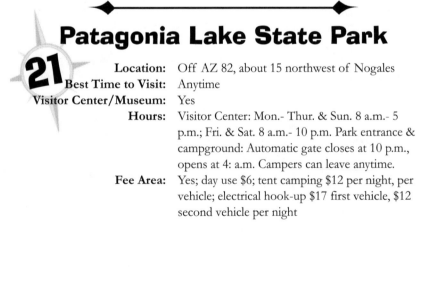

Location:	Off AZ 82, about 15 northwest of Nogales
Best Time to Visit:	Anytime
Visitor Center/Museum:	Yes
Hours:	Visitor Center: Mon.- Thur. & Sun. 8 a.m.- 5 p.m.; Fri. & Sat. 8 a.m.- 10 p.m. Park entrance & campground: Automatic gate closes at 10 p.m., opens at 4: a.m. Campers can leave anytime.
Fee Area:	Yes; day use $6; tent camping $12 per night, per vehicle; electrical hook-up $17 first vehicle, $12 second vehicle per night

Restroom:	Yes; barrier-free; showers available
Wheelchair/Stroller Access:	Yes; one handicapped camping site each in tent area and electrical hook-up sites
Drinking Water:	Yes
Picnic Area:	Yes
Lodging:	No
Camping:	Yes
Suitable for:	All ages
Notes/Tips:	Scheduled to open in late 1999, Sonoita Creek State Natural Area is a beautiful riparian area located only a few miles from Patagonia Lake. Contact Arizona State Parks for details.

In the deserts of southern Arizona, the blue waters of tiny Patagonia Lake seem out-of-place. The 2.5 mile-long lake is a favorite recreation site for Arizona boaters, anglers and water sport enthusiasts. Skiing, camping, boating, picnicking, hiking and fishing for bass, crappie, bluegill and catfish are popular activities.

Sonoita Creek State Natural Area

Sonoita Creek, totaling almost 5,000 acres, is Arizona's first major state natural area. A part of Arizona State Parks, and located within Patagonia Lake State Park, Sonoita Creek is a unique riparian preserve. State Parks will develop hiking trails and wildlife viewing areas along the creek and throughout the property. Environmental programs for all ages will be offered as well as research opportunities for universities. Designated as a *significant* riparian area, it is home to giant cottonwoods, willows, sycamores, and mesquites, nesting black hawks, and endangered species. At this time, however, only the Sonoita Creek State Natural Area Visitor Center, located in Patagonia State Park, is open to the public.

Patagonia Lake State Park, P.O. Box 274, Patagonia, AZ 85624, 520-287-6965

22 Nogales

Location: At the end of I-19, 15 miles south of Tumacacori

The largest border city in Arizona, Nogales is a fun day trip, even if you have visited other locations in Mexico. You'll find some excellent restaurants and cantinas. Many visitors enjoy browsing and shopping for clothing, furniture, jewelry and unique crafts. A shopper with a keen eye for quality can find some terrific bargains.

I suggest parking on the American side and walking across the border. The streets of Nogales, Sonora are narrow and very congested. Finding a parking place is a challenge.

Before visiting Nogales, contact the Nogales-Santa Cruz County Chamber of Commerce for a free information packet.

Nogales-Santa Cruz County Chamber of Commerce, Kino Park, Nogales, AZ, 85621, 520-287-3685, Fax: 520-287-3688, email: chamber1@dakotacom.net

23 Kitt Peak Observatory

Location:	Off AZ 386, 56 miles southwest of Tucson. See Notes/Tips
Best Time to Visit:	Late spring, summer, early fall; severe winter storms are common
Visitor Center/Museum:	Yes
Hours:	Daily 9 a.m.- 3:45 p.m.
Fee Area:	Tours are free; call for prices of special programs
Restroom:	Yes; barrier-free
Wheelchair/Stroller Access:	Yes; visitor center and portions of the walking trails
Drinking Water:	Yes
Picnic Area:	No
Lodging:	No

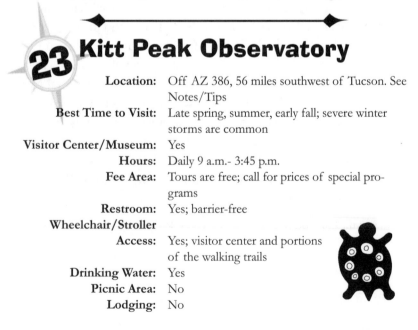

Camping:	No
Suitable for:	All ages; best for ages 8 & older
Notes/Tips:	Allow at least two hours for the drive from Tucson. The road is steep and narrow, but the views are spectacular. At almost 7,000 feet, be prepared with warm clothing. No food or gas stations available.

The world's largest collection of optical telescopes is located high above the Sonoran Desert under some of the finest night skies in the world. Kitt Peak Observatory is home to 22 optical and two radio telescopes

At Kitt Peak Visitor Center, you'll learn the history of optical astronomy and the role Kitt Peak has had in shaping astronomical research for the past four decades.

You can take a self-guided tour, or a free guided discovery that departs from the visitor center twice daily. Advanced programs, including family stargazing and over night adventures, are available with reservations.

National Optical Astronomy Observatories, P.O. Box 26732, Tucson, AZ 85726-6732

Kitt Peak Visitor Center, 520-318-8726, Recorded Information, 520-318-8200

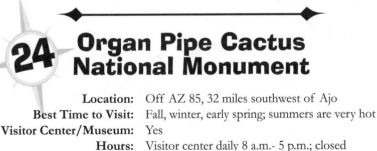

24 Organ Pipe Cactus National Monument

Location:	Off AZ 85, 32 miles southwest of Ajo
Best Time to Visit:	Fall, winter, early spring; summers are very hot
Visitor Center/Museum:	Yes
Hours:	Visitor center daily 8 a.m.- 5 p.m.; closed Christmas; loop drives & campgrounds 24 hrs.
Fee Area:	Yes; $4 per vehicle, good for 7 days; camping $8 per vehicle
Restroom:	Yes; barrier-free
Wheelchair/Stroller Access:	At visitor center only

Drinking Water:	Yes
Picnic Area:	Yes
Lodging:	No; nearest lodging in Ajo
Camping:	Yes; with pull-in sites for trailers; no showers or electrical hook-ups
Suitable for:	All ages
Notes/Tips:	This is a very remote, rugged area with limited services. Make sure your vehicle is in good condition and top-off the gas tank in Ajo. Overnight stays are best for experienced campers.

Organ Pipe Cacti are extremely rare in the United States, but common south of the border. The many arms of the organ pipe distinguish it for the saguaro. The largest concentration of organ pipe north of the border is found at the monument.

Camping, hiking and wildlife observation are very popular in this pristine desert environment. To get a close-up view of the cacti, however, you'll need to take one of the two loop drives that wind through the park.

Organ Pipe National Monument, Rt. 1, Box 100, Ajo, AZ 85321, 520-387-6849

Southern Arizona

Central Mountains
& Mogollon Rim Map

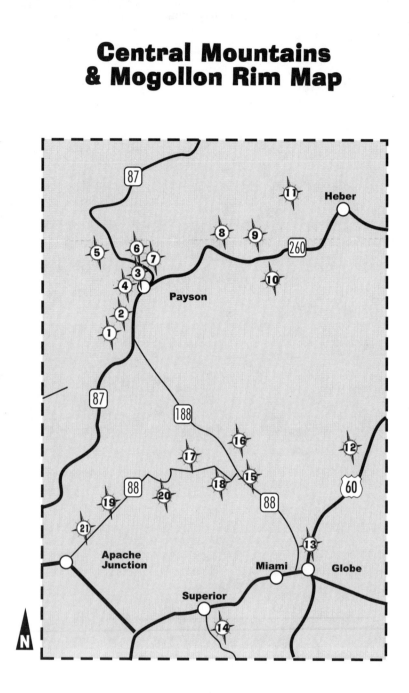

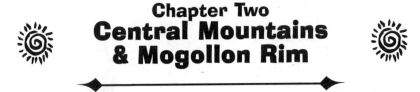

Chapter Two
Central Mountains
& Mogollon Rim

When schools recess for the summer, many desert dwellers begin an annual migration. Packing vehicles with camping gear and fishing tackle, families find temporary relief from the searing summer heat in Arizona's central mountains and on the Mogollon Rim.

In a land of towering mountains and old-growth pine forests, you'll find clear lakes and creeks stocked with catchable trout, primitive and full-service campgrounds, log cabins and friendly little towns.

On your discovery of the central mountains, you can explore a tropical paradise beneath an enormous bridge, feed hundreds of trout that are longer than your arm and go whitewater rafting through a spectacular gorge. You may even pick-up a few xeriscape tips for your yard when visiting Arizona's smallest state park.

If phantom gold mines, lost treasure and wilderness hiking suit your fancy, you'll be in your heaven exploring the legendary Superstition Mountains and a 1880s mining camp along the famous Apache Trail.

There are three main routes from desert communities to the cool central mountains and Mogollon Rim. Let's begin our discovery along the most heavily traveled road, AZ 87, The Beeline Highway, that leads to Payson. We'll backtrack a bit, making a loop on AZ 188 and I-60 and conclude our journey along the Apache Trail.

Barnhardt Hiking Trail

Location:	Trailhead (very visible sign) is 22 miles south and five miles west of Payson, off AZ 87. After leaving the highway, drive five miles on a dirt Forest Service Rd. to the parking lot
Best Time to Visit:	Early spring, fall; hot in the summer, cold & snow in the winter
Visitor Center/Museum:	No
Hours:	Hike during daylight only
Fee Area:	No
Restroom:	No
Wheelchair/Stroller Access:	No
Drinking Water:	No; see Notes/Tips
Picnic Area:	No
Lodging:	No
Camping:	No established sites
Suitable For:	Best for kids ages 6 yrs. and older
Notes/Tips:	Bring at least a quart of water (more is better) for everyone. Wear hiking boots, hats and sunglasses. Rattlesnake country - stay on trail

The Mazatzal (say "mad as hell" very quickly) Mountain Wilderness features numerous hiking trails through some of the best scenery Arizona has to offer. The Barnhardt Trail is one of the most beautiful and popular hiking destinations in this splendid wilderness.

The first part of the trail is level but rocky. As you begin a gradual ascent, the rocks disappear and the trail makes easy switchbacks along the side of a magnificent canyon. Far below, you'll hear and see a flowing stream and shimmering waterfalls. You might spot mule deer, different species of hawks or even a bald eagle.

Many hikers make the climb to a saddle between two mountains for a stunning view of the Mogollon Rim. But even if you turn around before reaching the saddle, you'll be rewarded with a great family adventure.

2 Payson

Location:	On AZ 87, about 80 miles northeast of Scottsdale
Best Time to Visit:	Year round

Just under a mile high and situated at the base of the Mogollon Rim, the lovely town of Payson is the gateway to Arizona's central mountains. Here you'll find all services including fine restaurants, numerous motels and resorts and even a gaming casino. If you plan on making Payson your headquarters, contact the Rim Country Regional Chamber of Commerce for helpful information.

Rim Country Regional Chamber of Commerce, Payson Office, P.O. Box 1380, Payson, AZ 85547, 928-474-4515

3 Rim Country Museum

Location:	On Green Valley Parkway in Payson
Best Time to Visit:	Anytime
Visitor Center/Museum:	Yes
Hours:	Noon-4 p.m. Wed.-Sun.; closed major holidays
Fee Area:	Yes; $3 ages 13 & older; $2.50 seniors; $2 students; ages 12 & under free
Restroom:	Yes; barrier free
Wheelchair/Stroller Access:	Yes; entire complex
Drinking Water:	Yes
Picnic Area:	Yes; at Green Valley Park
Lodging:	Available in Payson, Strawberry & Pine
Camping:	At Houston Mesa; see next entry
Suitable For:	All ages

Located in beautiful Green Valley Park, this fascinating museum focuses on the history of the Payson area. Exhibits feature the logging and mining industries, pre-historic and present day Native

American traditions, and Zane Grey, the renowned author of Western tales who once lived in the Payson area. Even the buildings are historic, dating to 1907. Trout fishing is available in the small lakes on park grounds for those with an urban fishing license.

Rim Country Museum, 700 Green Valley Parkway, Payson, AZ 85541, 928-474-3483.

Houston Mesa Campground

Location:	2 miles north of Payson off AZ 87. Turn right on Houston Mesa Rd. (FS 199)
Best Time to Visit:	Late spring, summer, early fall
Visitor Center/Museum:	No; camp host on site
Hours:	24 hrs. daily from Mar. 1- Nov. 30
Fee Area:	Yes; $12 per vehicle per night
Restroom:	Yes; barrier-free
Wheelchair/Stroller Access:	Yes; most sites, trails & roads
Drinking Water:	Yes
Picnic Area:	Yes
Lodging:	No
Suitable for:	All ages
Notes/Tips:	Very popular; make reservations

Family camping, going away, is the number one reason so many folks visit the cool central mountains. Near Payson, you'll find dozens of established campgrounds and many undeveloped sites. For those new to camping, or families that prefer some creature comforts without sacrificing the fun of an outdoor experience, Houston Mesa Campground is ideal.

Located on the outskirts of Payson (a 10-minutes drive if you need supplies) Houston Mesa features 75 sites for tent, trailer and RV camping, very clean restrooms with flushing toilets, sinks and mirrors, drinking water, showers ($1), amphitheater, dump station and equestrian area.

Houston Mesa Campground, c/o Tonto National Forest, Payson district, 1009 E. Hwy. 260, Payson, AZ 85541, 928-474-7900; or call: National Recreation Reservation Center, 800-280-2276

5 Tonto National Bridge State Park

Location:	Off AZ 87, 10 miles north of Payson
Best Time to Visit:	Late spring, summer early fall
Visitor Center/Museum:	Historic lodge & gift shop
Hours:	Apr.-Oct. 8 a.m.- 6 p.m.; Nov.-Mar. 9 a.m.- 5 p.m.; closed Christmas
Fee Area:	Yes; $6 per vehicle with group of 1-6; $12 per vehicle with group of 7-12; $6 for additional increments of six
Restroom:	Yes; barrier-free
Wheelchair/Stroller Access:	Rim trail, lodge and parking lot are accessible. Canyon trails aren't
Drinking Water:	Yes
Picnic Area:	Yes; shaded ramadas
Lodging:	No
Camping:	No
Suitable for:	All ages
Notes/Tips:	Do not climb under waterfall, on mossy rocks, high cliffs or in caves. Don't disturb vegetation. No swimming under Natural Bridge. Pets not permitted on hiking trails. Violating rules will result in a quick escort from the park.

The closest thing to a rain forest you're likely to find in Arizona, Tonto Natural Bridge State Park is a geological and visual wonder.

The forces of water and rock combined to form the world's largest natural travertine (limestone composite) bridge. The incredible arch is 183 ft. high, 150 ft. at its widest point and 400 ft. long. A spring near the top of the arch creates a constant waterfall that tumbles into Pine Creek. The moisture allows ferns and mosses, found no where else in Arizona, to flourish. Rainbow trout can be spotted swimming in the crystal clear water of Pine Creek.

Well maintained hiking trails lead from the top of the bridge down to Pine Creek and through the arch.

This is one of the prettiest spots in Arizona and shouldn't be missed.

Tonto Bridge Natural State Park, P.O. Box 1245, Payson, AZ 85547, 928-476-4202; Fax: 928-476-2264

6 Pine and Strawberry

Location:	Off AZ 87, 20 miles north of Payson
Best Time to Visit:	Late spring, summer (June for the cook-off and festival; see Notes/Tips), early fall
Visitor Center/Museum:	Yes; in historic buildings and Strawberry Schoolhouse
Hours:	N/A
Fee Area:	No
Restroom:	Yes
Wheelchair/Stroller Access:	Yes
Drinking Water:	Yes
Picnic Area:	Yes
Lodging:	No
Camping:	No
Suitable for:	All ages
Notes/Tips:	For cook-out & festival date, contact: Rim

Only two miles separate the charming and rapidly growing vacation communities of Pine and Strawberry. Pine is named for the surrounding pine timber country. Strawberry is named for the wild strawberries that grow in the area.

The tiny towns are famous for their chili cook-off and strawberry festival that are held on the same day in June. A shuttle provides transportation between the towns. I also suggest taking the interesting walking tour of historic buildings in both towns.

Country Regional Chamber of Commerce, Pine office, 928-476-3547

Strawberry Schoolhouse

7

Location:	On Fossil Creek Rd. in Strawberry, 2 miles west of Highway 87
Best Time to Visit:	Summer; closed to public during winter
Visitor Center/Museum:	The school itself is a museum
Hours:	Anytime to see building; call for hours when schoolhouse is open for tours
Fee Area:	No
Restroom:	Outdoor toilet
Wheelchair/Stroller Access:	Yes
Drinking Water:	No
Picnic Area:	Yes; a few tables in the shade of tall pines
Lodging:	In Strawberry, Pine, and Payson
Camping:	No
Suitable for:	All ages

The oldest school building in Arizona, this historic one-room log schoolhouse was built in 1885. The interior has been restored and furnished to resemble the original. Many of the wooden desks have names carved into the surface. The wood burning stove was the only way of heating the school during cold winter months. The legend of the mysterious thief is re-told on a tour of this charming schoolhouse.

Strawberry Schoolhouse, 928-476-3095; 928-476-4791 or 928-476-3375

8 Kohls Ranch Lodge

Location:	Off AZ 260, 17 miles east of Payson
Best Time to Visit:	Anytime
Visitor Center/Museum:	Yes; free maps & concierge service
Hours:	24 hrs. daily
Fee Area:	Yes; seasonal rates. Inquire when making reservations
Restroom:	Yes
Wheelchair/Stroller Access:	Yes
Drinking Water:	Yes
Picnic Area:	Yes
Camping:	No
Suitable for:	All ages
Notes/Tips:	Romantic get-away

Enjoy a little pampering in the wilderness? Kohls Ranch is the place. Tucked beneath towering pines, this small resort offers eight creekside cabins with decks, outdoor Jacuzzis and a fireplace. There are 41 lodge rooms with full kitchens, TV and a fireplace.

Hearty western cuisine is served daily for breakfast, lunch and dinner in the Zane Grey Dining Room. The legendary Cowboy Bar has been pouring for guests since 1920.

The ranch also features an outdoor pool, spa, putting green, sport court, fitness room, volleyball court, kid's playground barn, an 18-suite pet lodge for your four-legged friends and much more. On-property horseback riding and trout fishing are also popular.

Kohls Ranch Lodge, East Highway 260, Payson, AZ 85541, 800-331-5645 or 928-478-1211; Fax: 928-478-5055

Tonto Creek Fish Hatchery

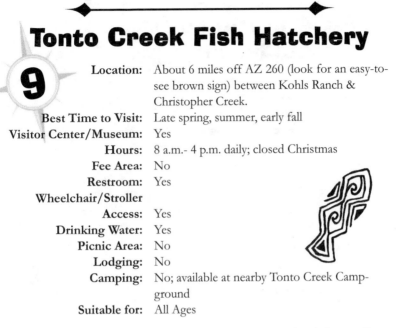

9

Location:	About 6 miles off AZ 260 (look for an easy-to-see brown sign) between Kohls Ranch & Christopher Creek.
Best Time to Visit:	Late spring, summer, early fall
Visitor Center/Museum:	Yes
Hours:	8 a.m.- 4 p.m. daily; closed Christmas
Fee Area:	No
Restroom:	Yes
Wheelchair/Stroller Access:	Yes
Drinking Water:	Yes
Picnic Area:	No
Lodging:	No
Camping:	No; available at nearby Tonto Creek Campground
Suitable for:	All Ages

With a growing number of anglers in the state, the Arizona Game & Fish Department operates a number of trout hatcheries throughout Arizona. One of the oldest and most productive is the Tonto Creek Hatchery. Located on the banks of beautiful Tonto Creek, the facility has not only produced millions of catchable rainbow trout, but it has survived several enormous floods and the devastating Dude Fire of June, 1990.

Even if you don't fish, I recommend visiting. You'll learn how the trout are hatched and raised, what they're fed and where they will eventually be stocked. Huge trout can be seen swimming in a pond located at the entrance to the complex. A quarter will buy a handful of fish food from a vending machine that will cause a trout feeding frenzy. Its quite a show.

Tonto Creek Hatchery, HC 2, Box 96-I, Payson, AZ 85541, 928-478-4200

10 Christopher Creek and Campground

Location:	Off AZ 260, 19 miles east of Payson
Best Time to Visit:	Late spring, summer, early fall
Visitor Center/Museum:	No
Hours:	Market: 7 a.m.- to at least 7 p.m.; campground: 24 hrs. daily Apr.-Oct.
Fee Area:	Campground: $11 per night
Restroom:	Market: yes; campground: yes
Wheelchair/Stroller Access:	Most roads & camping sites; restrooms, difficult but manageable
Drinking Water:	Yes
Picnic Area:	Yes
Lodging:	No
Camping:	43 sites; first-come first-serve. Tables, fire rings & grills
Suitable for:	All ages
Notes/Tips:	On summer weekends & holidays, campground is full by mid-Friday morning. Everyone ages 14 and older must have a valid Arizona fishing license to catch crawdads.

Christopher Creek is a tiny community that caters to campers and anglers. The Tall Pines Market is staffed by friendly, knowledgeable folks. The store carries basic necessities, some produce, packaged and frozen meat and dairy products. Fishing tackle and bait are also available. Located just two miles from Christopher Creek Campground, the market is the place to go if you need to re-supply.

Christopher Creek Campground is smaller then Houston Mesa and does not have all of the amenities. However, it located next to Christopher Creek. If the water level is sufficient, trout fishing can be very good. With a few feet of fishing line, a small hook and canned corn, kids can catch hundreds of crawdads (crayfish). When boiled, they taste like mini-lobster. See Notes/Tips.

Tall Pines Market, HC 2, Box 121L, Payson, AZ 85554, 928-478-4550; Christopher Creek Campground, 928-478-0188

11 Mogollon Rim Recreation Area

Location: The turnoff to the Rim Drive is 8 miles east of Christopher Creek, off AZ 260. Woods Canyon Lake is 5 miles from the turnoff

Best Time to Visit: Late spring, summer, early fall

Suitable for: All ages

Notes/Tips: There are so many campgrounds, marinas and recreation opportunities on the Mogollon Rim, they can't all be listed. For trip planning information, contact the Apache-Sitgreaves National Forest - Heber District or the Rim Country Regional Chamber of Commerce.

When you stop at Rim overlooks, be extremely cautious. There are sheer dropoffs and few guard rails. Don't get too close to the edge and keep a tight grip on your kids.

A 1,000-foot high escarpment, the Mogollon Rim is a defining Arizona landmark and one of the most popular outdoor recreation sites in the state. On the "Top of the Rim" you'll find a number of lakes, streams, primitive and established campgrounds.

Recreational activities include trout fishing, hiking, mountain biking, horseback riding, canoeing/rafting, wildlife viewing and boating. At Woods Canyon, the most popular lake on the Rim, you'll find a marina that offers boat and fishing tackle rentals, food and beverages. There is a fine visitor center at the Rim Lakes Recreation Center.

For spectacular views from the Rim, take the scenic Rim Drive Road.

Heber Ranger District, P.O. Box 968, Overgaard, AZ 85933, 928-535-4481

Rim Country Regional Chamber of Commerce-Payson Office, P.O. Box 1380, Payson, AZ 85547, 928-474-4515

12 Seneca Lake/Salt River Canyon

Location:	Off AZ 77, 30 miles northeast of Globe; see Notes/Tips
Best Time to Visit:	Spring
Visitor Center/Museum:	No
Hours:	Seneca Lake Campground - 24 hrs. daily
Fee Area:	Yes; $7 per night, individual; $10 per night, family. See Notes/Tips
Restroom:	Yes
Wheelchair/Stroller Access:	Limited to campground. Restroom not accessible
Drinking Water:	Yes
Picnic Area:	Yes
Lodging:	No
Camping:	Yes; see Notes/Tips
Suitable for:	Camping, all ages; rafting, see Notes/Tips
Notes/Tips:	AZ 77 is a steep, winding road; drive carefully. Scenery is breathtaking. Seneca Lake is situated on the San Carlos Indian Reservation. If planning to fish, you'll need to purchase a permit. Camping is primitive; best for experienced campers. Check with rafting outfitters regarding whitewater rafting age requirements.

Arizona is a land of many canyons. One is world famous, but the vast majority are tiny, deep gorges located in remote and rugged terrain. The Upper Salt River Canyon is one such place.

Camping and whitewater rafting are the best ways to experience the wonders of this incredible canyon. Seneca Lake is located near the rim of the canyon and offers primitive camping. At 6,000 feet, the water is cold enough to support a healthy population of catchable trout, including the rare Apache trout.

In early spring, runoff from melting snow causes a dramatic increase in the water flow of the Salt River. In the narrowest parts of the canyon, the roaring water draws hundreds of whitewater rafting enthusiasts.

I recommend taking at least one rafting trip on the Upper Salt River. Its a heart-pounding adventure in one of the prettiest spots in Arizona.

Seneca Lake Camping/Fishing, San Carlos Indian Reservation, Box 97, San Carlos, AZ 85550, 928-475-2343

Blue Sky Whitewater Rafting, 143 North High Street, Globe, AZ 85501, 928-425-5252 or 800-425-5253

Far Flung Adventures, 800-231-7238

13 Besh-Ba-Gowah Archaeological Park

Location:	1.25 miles from downtown Globe, off U.S. 60
Best Time to Visit:	Anytime
Visitor Center/Museum:	Yes
Hours:	Daily 9 a.m.- 5 p.m.; closed New Years, Thanksgiving, Christmas
Fee Area:	12 yrs & older, $3; under 12, free; 65 yrs & older, $2
Restroom:	Yes; barrier-free
Wheelchair/Stroller Access:	Yes; except upper rooms
Drinking Water:	Yes
Picnic Area:	Yes
Lodging:	No; available in Globe. Contact: Globe/Miami Chamber of Commerce, 1360 N. Broad St., P.O. Box 2539, Globe, AZ 85502, 928-425-4495 or 800-804-5623
Camping:	No
Suitable for:	All ages

Besh-Ba-Gowah (from Apache language, meaning "place of metal") is a multi-story ancient ruin unlike any other in Arizona. Because of the stability of the rock walls, you are encouraged to walk within the rooms of this 700 year old pueblo, climb ladders to the upper stories and examine utensils, pottery and furbishings that were used by the pre-Columbian Salado culture. Much of the huge complex has been excavated, but some rooms have been left undisturbed since the pueblo was mysteriously abandoned around A.D. 1400.

Begin your discovery at the remarkable visitor center/interpretive museum and adjoining ethnobotanical garden.

Besh-Ba-Gowah Archaeological Park, 150 N. Pine St., Globe, AZ 85501, 928-425-0320

14 Boyce Thompson Arboretum State Park

Location:	About 20 miles west of Globe, 3 miles east of Superior off U.S. 60
Best Time to Visit:	Spring, fall
Visitor Center/Museum:	Yes; including a plant sale greenhouse & gift shop
Hours:	8 a.m.- 5 p.m. daily; closed Christmas
Fee Area:	Yes; $5 per vehicle
Restroom:	Yes; barrier-free
Wheelchair/Stroller Access:	Yes; except one hiking trail
Drinking Water:	Yes
Picnic Area:	Yes; shaded by tall trees
Lodging:	No
Camping:	No
Suitable for:	All ages
Notes/Tips:	In October the arboretum conducts a huge plant sale that is extremely popular. Call for details.

Founded in 1924 by mining magnate William Boyce Thompson, this 300-acre state park is a mosaic of gardens and natural areas.

Nature trails wind through 35 acres of the grounds where you'll experience a year-round garden of many delights. Walk beneath majestic shade trees and between soaring canyon walls. Listen to the murmur of Queen Creek and the songs of many bird species. In the fall, you'll see the incredible red and golden autumn leaves, colorful fruit and berries. Spring bursts in with a profusion of yellow, orange and red desert wild flowers.

Boyce Thompson Arboretum State Park, 37615 E. Hwy. 60, Superior, AZ 85273-5100, 928-689-2811

15 Tonto National Monument

Location:	Off AZ 88, 35 miles west of Globe, 5 miles east of Roosevelt Lake
Best Time to Visit:	Early spring, late fall, winter
Visitor Center/Museum:	Yes
Hours:	Park/visitor center: 8 a.m.-5 p.m. daily; hiking trails close at 4 p.m.; closed Christmas
Fee Area:	$4 per vehicle
Restroom:	Yes; barrier-free
Wheelchair/Stroller Access:	Yes; at visitor center; ruins are not accessible
Drinking Water:	Yes
Picnic Area:	Yes; shaded ramadas
Lodging:	No
Camping:	No
Suitable for:	All ages
Notes/Tips:	It is unlawful to take or disturb archaeological or natural resources. Don't lean or climb on ruin walls. Pets must be leashed and under control. There are steep grades and uneven surfaces and visitors with heart or respiratory conditions should use caution. This is rattlesnake country; stay on trails and report a sighting to a park ranger.

Featuring two, 700 year-old cliff dwellings built by the pre-Columbian Salado culture, visiting Tonto National Monument is a must for amateur archaeologists and history buffs.

A half-mile self-guided trail climbs 350 vertical feet to the 19-room lower ruin. The magnificent 40-room upper ruin with views of Roosevelt Lake, may be visited only on a conducted tour and advanced reservations are required.

A tour of Tonto National Monument begins at the visitor center. Salado crafts and tools are exhibited here and an audio-visual program describes the setting and introduces Salado culture.

Tonto National Monument, P.O. Box 707, Roosevelt, AZ 85545, 928-467-2241

16 Theodore Roosevelt Lake and Marina

Location:	Off AZ 88, 30 miles northwest of Globe
Best Time to Visit:	Early spring, fall, winter
Visitor Center/Museum:	Yes
Hours:	Visitor center: daily 7:45- 4:30 p.m.; Roosevelt Lake Marina: Mon.-Fri. & Sun 7 a.m.-5:30 p.m.; Sat. 7 a.m.-6 p.m.; most recreation sites open year-round
Fee Area:	Yes; seasonal. Check with visitor center & marina
Restroom:	Yes; at visitor center, marina campgrounds & recreation sites
Wheelchair/Stroller Access:	Varies; contact the visitor center & marina
Drinking Water:	Yes
Picnic Area:	Yes
Lodging:	Yes; call for seasonal rates & reservations
Camping:	Yes; excellent facilities
Suitable for:	All ages

One of the world's biggest man-made lakes, Roosevelt Lake is the largest of the Salt River Project Reservoirs. Covering more than 19,000 acres when full, swimming, boating, fishing, water skiing and jet skiing are among the popular activities.

The recreational area also offers hiking, picnicking, sight-seeing and camping at outstanding full-service campgrounds. Sites worth seeing include Roosevelt Dam, Bermuda Flats and Windy Hill Recreation Sites.

Roosevelt Dam (named after President Theodore Roosevelt) is one of the world's largest masonry dams, standing 357 ft. tall. The Roosevelt Visitor Center offers a patio view of the lake as well as maps, gift items and books.

Roosevelt Visitor Center, Tonto Basin Ranger District, HC 02, Box 4800, Roosevelt, AZ 85545, 928-467-3200

Roosevelt Lake Marina, Box 458, Roosevelt, AZ 85545, 928-467-2245

Roosevelt RV Park & Motel, Box 736, Roosevelt, AZ 85545, 928-467-2888

Roosevelt Lake Resort, Rural Rt. 2, Box 901, Roosevelt, AZ 85546, 928-467-2276

17 — The Apache Trail

Location:	Between Apache Junction & Roosevelt Lake
Best Time to Visit:	Early spring, late fall, winter
Notes/Tips:	There are few services available. Your vehicle must be in good working order, especially tires, cooling system & brakes. Start with a full tank of gas and bring food and plenty of water. Between Apache Junction & Tortilla Flat the road is paved. Northeast of Tortilla Flat the road is unpaved (but in good condition) and narrow. Drive slowly and stay on your side of the road, particularly when approaching blind curves.

When President Theodore Roosevelt came to the dedication of the dam named in his honor, the presidential motorcade rumbled along the historic Apache Trail. In Roosevelt's words, the scenery along the Apache Trail was "the most sublimely beautiful panorama nature ever created." The road is in far better condition today, but the views are just as dramatic.

Depending on your direction of travel, The Apache Trail (AZ 88) begins or ends at Roosevelt Lake or Apache Junction. At just over 46 miles, you can make a round trip drive from either starting point in a single day.

Highlights of the drive include a ghost town, archaeological ruins, a state park and several historical points of interest. We'll stop at a few of the Campbell's favorite spots.

General information and driving conditions, contact: **Apache Junction Chamber of Commerce,** P.O. Box 1747, Apache Junction, AZ 85217-1747, 928-982-3141

If you would rather leave the driving to someone else, contact: **Apache Trail Tours,** P.O. Box 6146, Apache Junction, AZ 85278-6146, 928-982-7661

Tortilla Flat

Location:	28 miles southwest of Roosevelt Lake, 18 miles northeast of Apache Junction
Best Time to Visit:	Spring, fall, winter
Visitor Center/Museum:	The entire town is an historic museum
Hours:	Mon.-Fri. 9 a.m.-6 p.m.; Sat.-Sun. 8 a.m.-7 p.m.
Fee Area:	No
Restroom:	Yes; in the restaurant
Wheelchair/Stroller Access:	Yes; most of the boardwalks and establishments
Drinking Water:	Yes
Picnic Area:	No
Lodging:	No; planned for the future
Camping:	Yes; Oct.-May
Suitable for:	All ages

Often called the "biggest little town in Arizona," Tortilla Flat has a population of six, a bar, restaurant, general store/ice cream parlor, gift shop, and an official Post Office. A motel is also planned.

Once just a stagecoach stop along The Apache Trail, Tortilla Flat is an entertaining place to explore, especially for kids.

Alvin and Pam Ross own the entire town, including the Superstition Saloon and Restaurant. This is a good place to enjoy lunch. The hamburgers and sandwiches are huge and the prices are reasonable. The kids will marvel at the paper currency that covers every inch of the walls and ceiling. On your first visit, scribble a message on a dollar bill and have it added to collection.

Tortilla Flat, One Main St., Tortilla Flat, AZ 85290, 928-984-1776

Dolly Steamboat Cruises at Canyon Lake

19

Location:	Departs from Canyon Lake Marina, 14 miles northeast of Apache Junction
Best Time to Visit:	Early spring, fall, winter
Visitor Center/Museum:	No; restaurant & gift shop @ marina
Hours:	Departs Mon.-Fri. at noon; Sat.-Sun. noon & 2 p.m.; closed on Sun. June-Aug.
Fee Area:	13 & older $14; 6-12 $8; under 6 free
Restroom:	Yes; barrier-free
Wheelchair/Stroller Access:	Yes; call for arrangements
Drinking Water:	Yes
Picnic Area:	Yes
Lodging:	No
Camping:	Yes; for camping, private boating & services, contact: Canyon Lake Marina, P.O. Box 4978, Apache Junction, AZ 85278-4978, 928-944-6504
Suitable for:	All ages

Canyon Lake is appropriately named. This small reservoir is situated between spectacular towering cliffs. Numerous types of boats and yachts cruise the lake, but the oddest vessel is a double-decker paddle-wheeler named "The Dolly."

A cruise around Canyon Lake aboard the Dolly is a fun family adventure and a wonderful nature viewing experience.

Dolly cruises last about two hours. The experienced captain provides an interesting narrative, often pointing out soaring eagles, big horn sheep and other wildlife. There is plenty of room to move about. Snacks and beverages can be purchased, but you can bring a small cooler lunch.

Dolly Steamboat Cruises, P.O. Box 977, Apache Junction, AZ 85217-0977, 928-827-9144, Fax: 928-671-0483

Lost Dutchman State Park

20

Location:	5 miles northeast of Apache Junction
Best Time to Visit:	Early spring, late fall, winter
Visitor Center/Museum:	Yes
Hours:	Visitor Center 8 a.m.-5 p.m. daily except Christmas; campground open 24 hrs.
Fee Area:	Yes; $6 per vehicle up to 4 passengers; camping $12 per night
Restroom:	Yes; barrier-free
Wheelchair/Stroller Access:	Yes; with exception of some hiking trails
Drinking Water:	Yes
Picnic Area:	Yes; shaded ramadas
Lodging:	No
Camping:	Yes; 35 single family units, group area & dump station
Suitable for:	All ages

Care to try your luck at finding the legendary Lost Dutchman Gold Mine? Might just as well, since hundreds of other treasure hunters have tried and failed. Begin your search at the beautiful Lost Dutchman State Park.

Located at the base of the rugged Superstition Mountains, rumored to be the location of the Dutchman's mine, the park features excellent hiking trails rated from very easy to moderately difficult, equestrian trails and well maintained, full-service campgrounds.

In the early spring, if winter rains are sufficient to trigger germination, desert wild flowers bloom by the millions, creating a mosaic of colors that blankets the land for miles in all directions. Wildlife viewing and bird watching are also popular activities.

Lost Dutchman State Park, 6109 N. Apache Trail, Apache Junction, AZ 85219, 928-982-4485

Goldfield Ghost Town and Mining Camp

21

Location:	4 miles northeast of Apache Junction
Best Time to Visit:	Early spring, fall, winter
Visitor Center/Museum:	Yes
Hours:	Town: 10 a.m.-5 p.m.; railroad: Nov. 1-May 31 10 a.m.-5 p.m., Jun. 1-Oct. 31 10 a.m.-5 p.m. Thur.-Sun.
Fee Area:	fees charged for train ride, mine tour & other attractions
Restroom:	Yes; only barrier-free restroom is in the steakhouse
Wheelchair/Stroller Access:	Most of the town with exception of mine tour and several buildings
Drinking Area:	Yes
Picnic Area:	No
Lodging:	No
Camping:	No
Suitable for:	All ages

In the early 1900s, Goldfield was an authentic boom town and millions of dollars of gold were recovered from the nearby Mammoth Mine. Today, it's a family-friendly western theme park.

Parents will enjoy browsing in the boutiques, particularly the Giddy-Up Salsa Shop. Kids will have a hard time selecting an ice cream flavor in the Miner's Grill.

A tour of the make-believe gold mine is entertaining. I also suggest riding the scenic Superstition Railroad. The narrow-gauge steam engine offers wonderful views of the Superstition Mountains. Good western food is served at the Mammoth Steakhouse and Saloon.

Goldfield Ghost Town and Mining Camp, 4650 N. Mammoth Mine Rd., Goldfield, AZ 85219, 928-983-0333

Central Arizona Map

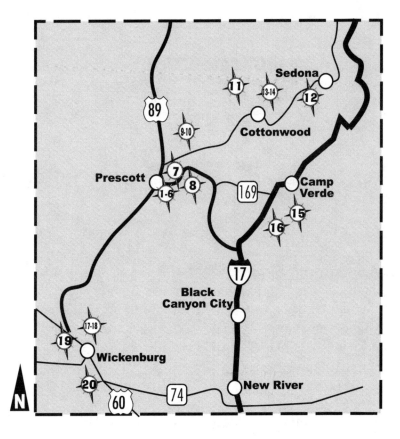

Chapter Three
Central Arizona

Ancient history, recent history and the future all come together in Arizona's Central Territory.

A predictable water source, rich planting soil and abundance of game provided the necessities for several pre-Columbian cultures that arrived in the Verde Valley of central Arizona more than 10,000 years ago.

The recent history of the central Arizona was written by explorers, prospectors and miners, cowboys and cavalrymen. With the arrival of the Europeans and Americans, the complexion of the Central Territory changed dramatically.

When rich veins of silver were discovered in the territory during the mid-1800s, raucous mining camps sprang up overnight. Reports of easy pickins fueled a population explosion. Jerome, with a population of 20,000, became the darling of the West and there was talk of statehood. Jerome being touted as the likely capital.

In 1864, President Lincoln established the Arizona Territory. But it was Prescott, not Jerome, that made pre-statehood history, having been chosen as the new capital of the Territory. Today, Prescott is the geographic and historic capital of central Arizona.

Using Prescott as a base camp, you can make leisurely side-trips to ancient ruins, old west forts, mining towns, secluded canyons and ghost towns.

1 Prescott

Location:	On AZ 69, 34 miles northwest of Cordes Jct.
Best Time to Visit:	Spring, summer , fall (vibrant fall colors)
Lodging:	Numerous hotels, motels & resorts; contact: Prescott Chamber of Commerce, 117 W. Goodwin St., Prescott, AZ 86303, 928-445-2000 or 800-266-7534
Camping:	Yes; including Potato Patch, Granite Basin and Mingus Mountain.

A complete listing of all the wonderful attractions in Prescott is beyond the scope of our Arizona discovery book. This Arizona community is deserving of repeat visits. Following the general information regarding Prescott, I've included a few of the Campbell family's favorite in-town attractions.

Contact: Prescott National Forest, 344 S. Cortez St., Prescott, AZ 86303, 928-771-4700

2 Courthouse Plaza

Boarded by Gurley and Goodwin streets to the north and south and Cortez and Montezuma streets to the west and east, Courthouse Plaza is the heart of Prescott. The old Yavapai County Courthouse stands in the middle of the plaza. Guarding the plaza is a bronze statue of Prescott's most famous citizen and renowned territorial lawman Bucky O'Neil, a Rough Rider who died assaulting San Juan Hill with Teddy Roosevelt. Stop at the Chamber of Commerce at the south end of the plaza and get a walking map of the town's Victorian neighborhood. Most attractions listed below are within walking distance of Courthouse Plaza.

3 Whiskey Row

Named for a score of saloons and brothels that lined Montezuma Street during territorial days, Whiskey Row was just as rowdy as Tombstone's notorious Allen Street. Today's Whiskey Row is a family place. Most of the old buildings now house boutiques, wonderful art galleries, western stores and charming ice cream parlors. Whiskey Row is located across the street from Courthouse Plaza.

4 Smoki Museum

Location:	On N. Arizona St., about one mile east of Sharlot Hall Museum
Visitor Center/Museum:	Yes
Hours:	May-Sept., Mon., Tues., Thurs.-Sat. 10 a.m. - 4 p.m., Sun. 1 p.m. - 4 p.m.; Oct., Fri.-Sun. 10 a.m. - 4 p.m. Usually closed Nov.-Apr.
Fee Area:	Yes; $2
Restrooms:	Yes; barrier-free
Wheelchair/Stroller Access:	Yes
Drinking Water:	Yes
Suitable for:	All ages; best for ages 8 yrs. and older

Built in 1935, this rustic log and rock cabin houses some priceless and fascinating Native American artifacts. Dating from the pre-Columbian period, the collection includes intricately woven rugs, beadwork and pottery.

Smoki Museum, 147 N. Arizona Street, Prescott, AZ 86303, 928-778-7754

5 Phippen Museum of Western Art

Location:	On Hwy. 89 N., about 5 miles northeast of Sharlot Hall Museum (you'll need to drive to this sight)
Visitor Center/Museum:	Yes
Hours:	Mon. & Wed.-Sat. 10 a.m.-4 p.m.; Sun. 1 p.m. - 4 p.m.
Fee Area:	Yes; $3
Restrooms:	Yes
Wheelchair/Stroller Access:	Yes
Drinking Water:	Yes
Suitable for:	All ages; best for ages 8 and older

This outstanding museum is considered one of the finest galleries of Western art in North America. Featured are paintings and bronze sculptures by renowned artist George Phippen. The many traveling art exhibits are first rate.

Phippen Museum of Western Art, 4701 Hwy. 89 N., Prescott, AZ 86303, 928-778-1385

About Sharlot Hall

Miss Sharlot Hall was truly a child of the frontier. Born in 1870, she traveled with her family from Kansas to the Arizona Territory in 1882. Mostly self-educated, Miss Hall's writings (both prose & poetry) are considered some of the most historically accurate records of life in early Arizona. In 1909, she was appointed territorial historian. In 1927, Miss Hall made an agreement with the state of Arizona to move her extensive collection of memorabilia and artifacts into the territorial Governor's Mansion. Today, the mansion is the focal point of a museum complex that bears her name. In 1981 Sharlot Hall became one of the first women elected to the Arizona Women's Hall of Fame.

Sharlot Hall Museum

6

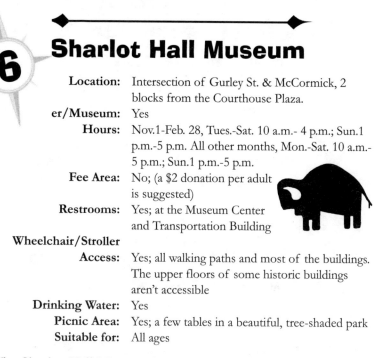

Location:	Intersection of Gurley St. & McCormick, 2 blocks from the Courthouse Plaza.
er/Museum:	Yes
Hours:	Nov.1-Feb. 28, Tues.-Sat. 10 a.m.- 4 p.m.; Sun.1 p.m.-5 p.m. All other months, Mon.-Sat. 10 a.m.- 5 p.m.; Sun.1 p.m.-5 p.m.
Fee Area:	No; (a $2 donation per adult is suggested)
Restrooms:	Yes; at the Museum Center and Transportation Building
Wheelchair/Stroller Access:	Yes; all walking paths and most of the buildings. The upper floors of some historic buildings aren't accessible
Drinking Water:	Yes
Picnic Area:	Yes; a few tables in a beautiful, tree-shaded park
Suitable for:	All ages

The Sharlot Hall Museum is not a museum in the true sense of the word. Located in downtown Prescott, this is actually a three-acre wooded park where you'll spend just as much time outside as you will exploring the historic buildings and exhibits. The park is also a charming place for a family picnic.

In all, there are 16 buildings/exhibits on the grounds, including the Museum Center, the park's focal point. Allow a half-day to take in all of the sights.

Don't miss the Blacksmith Shop, Locomotive display, Fort Misery, Ranch House, Transportation Building and the Country Schoolhouse.

Sharlot Hall Museum, 415 W. Gurley St., Prescott, AZ 86301, 928-445-3122

7 Granite Dells Recreation Park

Location:	Off Highway 89, four miles north of Prescott
Best Time to Visit:	Spring, summer, fall
Visitor Center/Museum:	No
Hours:	Anytime for fishing, hiking, and boating at the lake. Seasonal for day use & camping; call for current information
Fee Area:	Yes for day use & camping; call for seasonal rates
Restrooms:	Yes
Wheelchair/Stroller Access:	At campground & playground; some short hiking trails have limited access
Drinking Water:	Yes
Picnic Area:	Yes; some shaded ramadas
Lodging:	Not on site; available in Prescott
Camping:	Yes
Suitable for:	All ages
Notes/Tips:	Because of numerous submerged rocks, **_diving is prohibited_**, but swimming is allowed. Use caution when hiking and/or rock climbing. Kids should be supervised.

Granite Dells Recreation Park is a surrealistic jumble of weathered granite boulders and steep cliffs. The construction of a dam across Granite Creek created a small lake at the Dells. Fishing, swimming, and boating are all popular activities. Hiking through the maze of rocks is also popular.

The campground is clean, and features modern restrooms, picnic areas, and a kids playground.

Granite Dells Recreation Park, Point of Rocks Campground, 928-445-9018

Lynx Lake

Location:	On Walker Road, 10 miles south of Highway 69
Best Time to Visit:	Spring, summer, early fall
Visitor Center/Museum:	No
Hours:	Fishing anytime; campgrounds open Mar.-Nov.
Fee Area:	No
Restrooms:	Yes; at campgrounds & marina store
Wheelchair/Stroller Access:	Limited to campgrounds and boat dock
Drinking Water:	Yes
Picnic Area:	Yes
Lodging:	No
Camping:	Yes; two large campgrounds with modern restrooms
Suitable for:	All ages
Notes/Tips:	Very popular camping destination during the summer. Campgrounds are usually full by early Friday morning; even earlier on long holiday weekends. Make reservations.

Beautiful Lynx Lake is situated in the tall pines where summer temperatures are at least 20 degrees cooler than the desert areas. Trout fishing, camping, boating, and hiking are all popular activities. The campgrounds feature tent and RV sites, fire rings, charcoal grills, and picnic tables. The Lynx Lake Marina includes a grocery store and tackle shop. Boat rentals are available.

Lynx Lake, Prescott National Forest, 344 S. Cortez St.., Prescott, AZ 86303, 928-771-4700

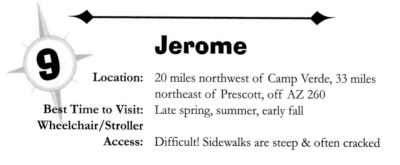

Jerome

Location:	20 miles northwest of Camp Verde, 33 miles northeast of Prescott, off AZ 260
Best Time to Visit:	Late spring, summer, early fall
Wheelchair/Stroller Access:	Difficult! Sidewalks are steep & often cracked

Picnic Area:	Yes; at Jerome City Park
Lodging:	Yes; but limited. Contact: Jerome Chamber of Commerce, Box K, Jerome, AZ 86331, 928-634-2900
Camping:	See Prescott
Notes/Tips:	Wear hiking boots or comfortable walking shoes. Jackets needed after sundown.

Before the turn of the century, when silver was "king", Jerome was the most populated city between St. Louis and San Francisco. Built on the side of Cleopatra Hill, Jerome was the hub of the Arizona Territory. But when the silver mines played out, eastern investors stopped pouring money into the dry holes. By 1950, there were less than 100 permanent residents in the city.

In the mid 1960s, the counter-culture discovered Jerome, triggering a renaissance. Writers, painters and craft artisans converted old brothels, saloons and dry goods stores into studios and gift shops. Working hand-in-hand with the "old timers", Jerome was re-born.

A walking tour of Jerome is the best way to experience the charm of this old/new town. Besides the many quaint shops that are worth investigating, don't pass up the three mining museums or Jerome State Historic Park (see below).

Jerome State Historic Park

10

Location:	On State Park Rd., off AZ 89A
Visitor Center/Museum:	Yes
Hours:	Daily 8 a.m.-5 p.m.
Fee Areas:	Yes; $3
Restrooms:	Yes; barrier-free
Wheelchair/Stroller Access:	Yes; but limited to 1st floor
Drinking Water:	Yes
Suitable For:	All ages

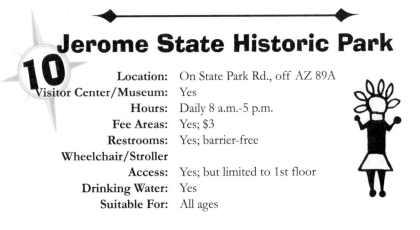

The main attraction at Jerome State Historic Park is the wonderful museum that occupies the old mansion of Jerome's mining king Dr. James "Rawhide Jimmy" Douglas, Jr. The house was built in 1917, five years after Douglas purchased The Little Daisy Mine, Jerome's most profitable glory hole. The tools and heavy equipment that were once used at the Little Daisy are remarkable reminders of a bygone era. A terrific video details the history of Jerome. Views from the mansion are spectacular; you can see the San Francisco Peaks, the Mogollon Rim and the red rocks of Sedona.

Jerome State Historic Park, State Park Rd., Jerome, AZ 86331, 928-634-5381

Verde Canyon Railroad

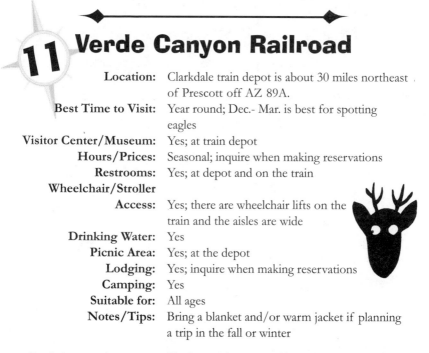

Location:	Clarkdale train depot is about 30 miles northeast of Prescott off AZ 89A.
Best Time to Visit:	Year round; Dec.- Mar. is best for spotting eagles
Visitor Center/Museum:	Yes; at train depot
Hours/Prices:	Seasonal; inquire when making reservations
Restrooms:	Yes; at depot and on the train
Wheelchair/Stroller Access:	Yes; there are wheelchair lifts on the train and the aisles are wide
Drinking Water:	Yes
Picnic Area:	Yes; at the depot
Lodging:	Yes; inquire when making reservations
Camping:	Yes
Suitable for:	All ages
Notes/Tips:	Bring a blanket and/or warm jacket if planning a trip in the fall or winter

In Arizona, there are still places that are off the beaten path and remain relatively undisturbed by man. One such place is the magnificent Verde Canyon. Without a 4-wheel drive vehicle and an adventurous spirit, discovering the hidden wonders of Verde Canyon would be next to impossible. That is, unless you ride the rails on the Verde Canyon Railroad.

The Verde Canyon Railroad is an excursion train that makes a 40-mile round trip wilderness run from the town of Clarkdale to the Perkinsville Junction. From climate-controlled cars or open-air gondolas, you might spot mule deer, javelina, mountain lions, and very rare black hawks. But the big draw is the opportunity to see bald and golden eagles that nest on the canyon cliffs above the Verde River.

Verde Canyon Railroad, 300 N. Broadway, Clarkdale, AZ 86324, 800-293-7245

12 Tuzigoot National Monument

Location:	Three miles north of Cottonwood and just east of Clarkdale
Best Time to Visit:	Year round
Visitor Center/Museum:	Yes
Hours:	Daily 8 a.m.-5 p.m.; closed Christmas
Fee Area:	Yes; $2 per person
Restrooms:	Yes; barrier-free
Wheelchair/Stroller Access:	Yes; in visitor center/museum, restroom and along a gravel path that winds around the complex.
Drinking Water:	Yes
Picnic Area:	Yes; shaded ramadas
Lodging:	Yes; in Clarkdale. Contact:, Clarkdale Chamber of Commerce, Box 161, Clarkdale, AZ 86324, (928) 634-3382
Camping:	See Prescott
Suitable for:	All ages
Notes/Tips:	Wear hiking boots or comfortable walking shoes

Tuzigoot (Apache for "crooked water") is the impressive remnant of a Sinaguan culture fortress and village. Built between A.D.1125 and 1400, it crowns the summit of a hill that rises 120 feet above the Verde Valley and River.

The labor involved in constructing the site had to be back-breaking. The entire complex is rock and adobe mortar. Even at two stories and with 77 ground floor rooms, there were few doors; entry was by way of ladders through small openings in the roof.

The interpretative museum is first rate and the artifact collection is outstanding. This is also one of the few pre-Columbian sites in Arizona where visitors are allowed to explore interior rooms. The view from the top is spectacular.

Tuzigoot National Monument, P.O. Box 68, Clarkdale, AZ 86324, 928-634-5564

13 Montezuma Castle National Monument

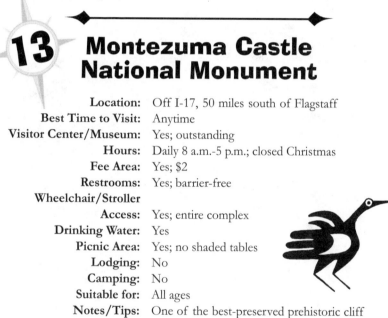

Location:	Off I-17, 50 miles south of Flagstaff
Best Time to Visit:	Anytime
Visitor Center/Museum:	Yes; outstanding
Hours:	Daily 8 a.m.-5 p.m.; closed Christmas
Fee Area:	Yes; $2
Restrooms:	Yes; barrier-free
Wheelchair/Stroller Access:	Yes; entire complex
Drinking Water:	Yes
Picnic Area:	Yes; no shaded tables
Lodging:	No
Camping:	No
Suitable for:	All ages
Notes/Tips:	One of the best-preserved prehistoric cliff dwelling ruins in North America

The ancient Sinagua culture began building this magnificent cliff dwelling around A.D. 1100. When it was abandoned around 1400, the structure was a five-story, 20-room complex tucked into a recess of a cliff, a 100 feet above a fertile valley. The Sinagua were farmers and Beaver Creek provide a reliable source of irrigation water.

United States army scouts were the first white men to discover the forgotten ruins. Because the construction was so intricate, they mistakenly thought the complex was built by the Aztec culture. They named the ruins after Aztec ruler Moctezoma (Montezuma).

Montezuma Castle National Monument, P.O. Box 219, Camp Verde, AZ 86322, 928-567-3322

Montezuma Well

14

Location:	From Montezuma Castle, take I-17 north just one exit. The well is about four miles east of the freeway
Best Time to Visit:	Anytime
Visitor Center/Museum:	No; ranger booth only
Hours:	Daily 8 a.m.-5 p.m.; closed Christmas
Fee Area:	Yes; $2 per person
Restrooms:	Yes
Wheelchair/Stroller Access:	No
Drinking Water:	Yes
Picnic Areas:	Yes; no shaded tables
Lodging:	No
Camping:	No
Suitable for:	All ages
Notes/Tips:	Although railings are in place at rim overlooks, use extreme caution. Keep a tight grip on kids. Some hiking required; wear appropriate shoes or boots.

Montezuma Well is not a hole in the ground from which one draws water. The Well is, in fact, a large pond or sinkhole surrounded by limestone cliffs.

From the rim of the well, you'll discover Sinagua and Hokokam cliff dwellings. You might spot ring-tailed cats, raccoons or even a mountain lion.

The pond is between 55 & 60 feet deep and measures about 365 feet across. The water temperature remains a constant 76 degrees. Kids will delight in watching the several different species of turtles that live in the well.

A short trail leads from the rim down to the banks of Beaver Creek, a perfect spot for a picnic.

In 1994, this writer contacted the National Park Service seeking permission to scuba dive the well. Citing archaeological and environmental sensitivity concerns, permission was denied.

Address inquiries to Montezuma Castle National Monument, 928-567-4521

15 Fort Verde State Historic Park

Location:	Off I-17 at any of the three Camp Verde exits; follow signs
Best Time to Visit:	Anytime
Visitor Center/Museum:	Yes; excellent displays
Hours:	Daily 8 a.m.- 4:30 p.m.
Fee Area:	Yes; $3 per person
Restrooms:	Yes; barrier-free
Wheelchair/Stroller Access:	Yes; entire facility
Drinking Water:	Yes
Picnic Area:	Yes
Lodging:	Yes; contact: Camp Verde Chamber of Commerce, 435 S. Main St., Box 1665, Camp Verde, AZ 86322, 928-567-9294
Camping:	No
Suitable for:	All ages; best for kids studying Arizona history

Built between 1871 - 1873 as the third of three military outposts designed to protect citizens of the Verde Valley from Apache and Yavapai raids, Fort Verde contained more than twenty buildings arranged around a parade ground. It was never a walled fortress and was never attacked.

Two companies of cavalry and two of infantry were stationed at the fort. Most of the soldier's time was spent building a dam, irrigation canals and a wagon road, later named the Crook Road after General George Crook.

In 1882, after the last major battle with renegade Apaches at Big Dry Wash, Fort Verde became less important and was abandoned in 1891.

Established in 1970, 10-acre Fort Verde State Historic Park includes a museum, three officers quarters, the administration building and a portion of the parade ground.

Camp Verde State Historic Park, P.O. Box 397, Camp Verde, AZ 86322, 928-567-3275

Arcosanti

16

Location:	65 miles north of Phoenix off I-17
Best Time to Visit:	Spring, fall
Visitor Center/Museum:	Yes
Hours:	Daily 9 a.m.-5 p.m.; guided tours hourly 10 a.m.-4 p.m.
Fee Area:	No; $5 donation appreciated
Restrooms:	Yes; barrier-free
Wheelchair/Stroller Access:	Yes
Drinking Water:	Yes
Picnic Area:	Yes; shaded ramadas
Lodging:	No
Camping:	No
Suitable For:	All ages

"Arcology" is a term coined by visionary Italian architect Paolo Soleri to describe the concept of architecture and ecology working as one integral process to produce new urban habitats.

Arcosanti is a totally energy-independent town that features desert-rock retaining walls and solar greenhouses that inspire ideas for dramatic Southwestern design and ecologically sensitive living. If you like wind-chimes, you will appreciate watching craftsman make the hand-cast bronze bells that have made Arcosanti world famous.

Arcosanti, HC 74, Box 4136, Mayer, AZ 86333, 928-632-7135

17 Wickenburg

Location:	65 miles northwest of Phoenix, off U.S. 60
Best Time to Visit:	Spring , fall
Lodging/Camping:	Yes; contact: Wickenburg Chamber of Commerce, 216 N. Frontier Street, Wickenburg, AZ 85390, 928-684-5479

Wickenburg enjoys a wonderful history dating back to 1863 when German immigrant Henry Wickenburg made the richest gold strike in the Arizona Territory. Wickenburg's Vulture Mine produced enough gold to finance the Northern Army during the Civil War. In fact, the mine was still producing gold in 1942 when the government decided that gold mining was not essential to the World War Two effort, and the mine was closed.

Wickenburg is a growing community that boasts a wonderful western museum. On the outskirts of Wickenburg you can also discover a terrific ghost town and a stunning riparian wildlife preserve.

18 Desert Caballeros Western Museum

Location:	One block west of traffic light & intersection of U.S. 60 & U.S. 93
Visitor Center/Museum:	Yes
Hours:	Mon.-Sat.10 a.m.-5 p.m.; Sun. noon - 4 p.m.; closed New Year's Day, Easter, July 4, Thanksgiving & Christmas
Fee Area:	Yes; $4 adults; under 6 free
Restrooms:	Yes; barrier-free
Wheelchair/Stroller Access:	Yes
Drinking Water:	Yes

Lodging/Camping:	Yes; see Wickenburg
Suitable for:	All ages

Considered by many to be one of the finest museums in the Southwest, Desert Caballeros Western Museum features western art, period rooms, Native American art, miniature dioramas, minerals and gems and at least 12 temporary exhibitions.

Works by Frederic Remington and Charles Russell capture the work and romance of the cowboy. The Native American gallery features excellent examples of Navajo weaving and jewelry, Hopi kachinas, Apache baskets and ancient Anasazi pottery.

Desert Caballeros Western Museum, 21 N. Frontier St., Wickenburg, AZ 85390, 928-684-2272

Vulture Mine & Ghost Town/Wickenburg

19

Location:	Drive through Wickenburg on U.S. 60. Turn left on Vulture Mine Rd. & go about 12 miles to the mine.
Best Time to Visit:	Spring, fall
Visitor Center/Museum:	Yes
Hours:	Daily 8 a.m.-4 p.m. during winter months. Contact Wickenburg Chamber of Commerce for specifics
Fee Area:	Yes; $2 per person
Restrooms:	Yes
Wheelchair/Stroller Access:	No
Drinking Water:	Yes; at visitor center
Picnic Area:	Yes; no shaded tables
Lodging/Camping:	See Wickenburg
Suitable for:	Best for ages 5 yrs. and older
Notes/Tips:	Wear hiking boots or good walking shoes. Rattlesnake territory - stay on the trail

The site of Henry Wickenburg's fabulous gold strike, the historic mine offers a peek of yesteryear on a self-guided tour of the remaining mining camp buildings and mining operations headquarters.

On the one-mile hike, you'll visit a blacksmith shop, power plant, bunk house, saloon and assay office. Don't miss Henry Wickenburg's original home and the old hanging tree where 18 gold robbers met their fate.

Vulture Mine & Ghost Town (no on-site contact)
Contact the Wickenburg Chamber of Commerce

◆————————————◆

Hassayampa River Preserve

20

Location:	Off U.S. 60 @ mile marker 114; 3 miles south of Wickenburg
Best Time to Visit:	Spring, fall
Visitor Center/Museum:	Yes; outstanding facility
Hours:	Sept.16-May 14, Wed.-Sun. 8 a.m.-5 p.m.; May 15-Sept. 15, 6 a.m.-noon
Fee Area:	No; $5 donation appreciated
Restrooms:	Yes; barrier-free
Wheelchair/Stroller Access:	Yes; at visitor center & most portions of walking trails
Drinking Water:	Yes
Picnic Area:	Yes; both public and private.
Lodging:	No; available in Wickenburg
Camping:	No
Suitable for:	All ages
Notes/Tips:	Ideal location for introducing kids to birding and wildlife watching

Hassayampa, an Apache word that means "upside down river," is a unique desert riparian wilderness that is owned and managed by The Nature Conservancy.

On a walking tour of this jungle-like nature preserve, you might encounter a raccoon, javelina, a bobcat, mule deer or a ring-tailed cat. Mountain lions also frequent the area. Two, half-mile loop trails are self-guided nature walks suitable for the entire family. Include Hassayampa on your must see list.

Hassayampa River Preserve, Box 1162, Wickenburg, AZ 85358, 928-684-2772

Phoenix Environs Map

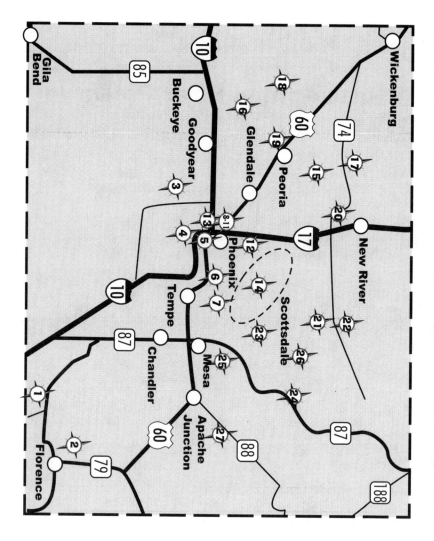

Chapter Four
Phoenix Environs

Located in the center of a 1,000-square-mile valley, the Phoenix metropolitan area is one of the fastest growing regions in the United States. Over half of Arizona's population reside in the ever-expanding state capital and its even faster growing suburbs. Phoenix is also the seat of Maricopa County, which in itself, encompasses an area larger than several New England states.

The Valley of the Sun, or simply the Valley, as the metro area is commonly called, offers a wide variety of activities, attractions and entertainment. You can find outstanding restaurants, plush resorts, hundreds of championship golf courses, desert mountain parks featuring excellent hiking and biking trails and exciting collegiate and professional sports teams.

There are so many things to see, experience and discover in the Valley of the Sun, I had to make tough decisions about what to include on these few pages. But we need to start somewhere.

In the southern most part of the Valley, we'll discover a 1,000 year-old mansion and the magnificent territorial home of a former governor and U.S. Senator. East of Phoenix, let's put on some grubby cloths and take a leisurely float down the Salt River. West of town, we'll literally feel the ground shake when the fighter jockeys go to afterburners.

Miles of hiking trails in city and county parks wait to be explored. In Phoenix's historic district, we'll investigate a world renowned southwestern museum and a fascinating science center. Near Tempe, home of the Arizona State University Sun Devils, a desert garden and world-class zoo await our arrival. Let's also visit an old gold mine and share a few laughs with a gal named Gabby.

Phoenix Visitor Information: Phoenix and Valley of the Sun Convention and Visitors Bureau, Arizona Center, 400 E. Van Buren St., Suite 600, Phoenix, AZ 85004, 602-254-6500
or
Arizona Office of Tourism, 2702 N. 3rd. St., Suite 4015, Phoenix, Az 85004, 602-230-7733 or 800-842-8257

1 Casa Grande National Monument

Location:	In Coolidge, on AZ 287
Best Time to Visit:	Spring, fall, winter
Visitor Center/Museum:	Yes
Hours:	Daily 8 a.m.-5 p.m.; closed Christmas
Fee Area:	16 & up $2; under 16 free
Restroom:	Yes; barrier free
Wheelchair/Stroller Access:	Yes; entire facility
Drinking Water:	Yes; bring water bottles
Picnic Area:	Yes
Lodging:	No
Camping:	No
Suitable for:	All ages

Casa Grande is an ancient Hohokam ruin that archaeologists still can't figure out. What was it? Located on a open plain and exposed to the elements for seven centuries, Casa Grande may have been a temple or palace, chief's home or an astrological observatory.

In 1694, Jesuit missionary Eusebio Francisco Kino became the first European to lay eyes on Casa Grande (Spanish for Big House). In 1918, the site was designated a national monument.

You can take a self-guided loop walk to the adobe ruins of the Big House and adjoining structures in the huge village. Be certain to visit the circular ball court that looks remarkably similar to courts found far to the south in central Mexico. Before beginning a tour of this archaeological treasure, spend time in the impressive visitor center that features interpretive exhibits and Hohokam artifacts. Allow 2 hours for this "must see" monument.

Casa Grande National Monument, 1100 Ruins Dr., Coolidge, AZ 85228, 520-723-3172

◆————————————◆

2 McFarland State Historic Park

Location:	In Florence, off U.S. 89 & AZ 287
Best Time to Visit:	Anytime
Visitor Center/Museum:	Yes
Hours:	Thur.-Mon. 8 a.m.-5 p.m.; closed Tues., Wed. & Christmas
Fee Area:	Yes; 14 & up $3; 7-13 $2; under 7 free
Restroom:	Yes; barrier free
Wheelchair/Stroller Access:	Yes
Drinking Water:	Yes
Picnic Area:	Yes
Lodging:	No; available in Florence
Camping:	No
Suitable for:	All ages; best appreciated by kids studying Arizona history

The original adobe structure at McFarland State Historic Park in historic Florence stood as the Pinal County Courthouse from 1878-91. A larger building, once the home of Ernest W. McFarland who began his career in law and politics in Pinal County and then went on to hold the highest office in each branch of Arizona Government, features his vast collection of memorabilia and historic artifacts.

Inside, view the many exhibits and displays depicting a bygone era when Florence was a hub of activity.

McFarland State Historic Park, P.O. Box 109, Florence, AZ 85232, 520-868-5216

❸ South Mountain Park

Location:	Main access point is at the south end of Central Ave. in Phoenix
Best Time to Visit:	Early spring, late fall, winter
Visitor Center/Museum:	An activity complex is located at the park entrance on Central Ave.
Hours:	Mon.-Sat. 9 a.m.-5: p.m.; Sun. noon-5 p.m.; hours can be extended, call for details
Fee Area:	No
Restroom:	Yes; at activity center and picnic ramadas. They are barrier-free. No facilities on hiking trails
Wheelchair/Stroller Access:	Limited to picnic areas and short portions of some trails
Drinking Water:	Yes; see Notes/Tips
Picnic Area:	Yes; sites can be reserved
Lodging:	No
Camping:	No
Suitable for:	All ages
Notes/Tips:	Because the trails are open to hikers, cyclists and equestrians, learn and obey right-of-way etiquette; ask a ranger for an explanation of right-of-way signs found along the trails.

This is rattlesnake territory. Stay on trails and don't step or reach where you can't see. Some trails are very long, traverse rugged terrain and are confusing, especially in bad weather. Obtain maps at activity center and don't push your limits. **Always carry at least a quart of water per person, more is better.** Wear hiking boots or sturdy shoes and hats.

Hiking, picnicking and spectacular distant views draw thousands of visitors annually to South Mountain, the world's largest municipal park.

The park area is reputed to have been claimed for Spain in 1539 by legendary missionary and explorer Father Marcos de Niza. His inscription (authenticity remains questionable) can be found on a rock off Pima Canyon Road.

In the 16,000-acre park, there are at least 15 maintained hiking trails totaling 40 miles. All trails are open to mountain bikers, hikers and equestrian riders (see Notes/Tips). Park rangers can help you select a hike that leads to a petroglyph site, one of more than 200 discovered to date.

Equipped with drinking water, electricity, toilets and firepits, picnic ramadas will accommodate up to 3,100 people. Sites can be reserved.

South Mountain Park, 10919 S. Central Ave., Phoenix, AZ 85040, 602-495-0222

4 Mystery Castle

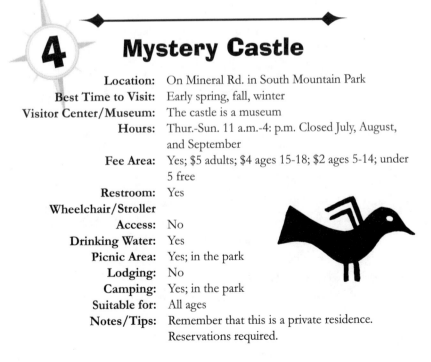

Location:	On Mineral Rd. in South Mountain Park
Best Time to Visit:	Early spring, fall, winter
Visitor Center/Museum:	The castle is a museum
Hours:	Thur.-Sun. 11 a.m.-4: p.m. Closed July, August, and September
Fee Area:	Yes; $5 adults; $4 ages 15-18; $2 ages 5-14; under 5 free
Restroom:	Yes
Wheelchair/Stroller Access:	No
Drinking Water:	Yes
Picnic Area:	Yes; in the park
Lodging:	No
Camping:	Yes; in the park
Suitable for:	All ages
Notes/Tips:	Remember that this is a private residence. Reservations required.

When Mary Lou Gulley was a little girl, she seldom saw her father. But her dad made one promise to his daughter that he kept. He built a magical castle for her.

Mr. Boyce Gulley constructed the huge fortress from almost anything he could find. This visually overwhelming castle includes 18 rooms with 13 fireplaces, 90 portholes, and a grotto. Mary Lou, who still lives at the castle, leads the tours..

Mystery Castle, 800 E. Mineral Rd., South Mountain Park, Phoenix, AZ 85040, 602-268-1581

5 Pueblo Grande Ruins and Museum

Location:	On the southeast corner of Washington & 44th Streets
Best Time to Visit:	Early spring, fall, winter
Visitor Center/Museum:	Yes
Hours:	Mon.-Sat. 9 a.m.-4:45 p.m.; Sun. 1 p.m.-4:45 p.m.; closed major holidays
Fee Area:	Yes; 18 & up $2; 6-17 $1; under 6 free
Restroom:	Yes; barrier free
Wheelchair/Stroller Access:	Yes; entire facility
Drinking Water:	Yes
Picnic Area:	Yes; shaded ramadas
Lodging:	No
Camping:	No
Suitable for:	All ages

Caught in a daily gridlock, frustrated commuters creep along Interstate 10, seldom giving a passing glance at the ancient ruins. Every day, 1,000 commercial jets land or take off within sight of the adobe walls. The contrast between a very modern city and an 800 year-old Hohokam village is stunning.

Located in the heart of Phoenix, Pueblo Grande Ruins and Museum features a fascinating interpretive center and easy hiking trails. The ruins, platform mounds and remains of a ball court are entered through the museum that houses artifacts such as tools, pottery and shell jewelry. Take an easy self-guided tour or make reservations for a ranger-guided walk.

The only national landmark in Phoenix, the park also offers a number of seasonal programs for kids and adults and unique tours to other ruins in the Southwest and Mexico.

Pueblo Grande Ruins & Museum, 4619 E. Washington St., Phoenix, Az 85034, 602-495-0901

6 The Phoenix Zoo

Location:	In Papago Park, off N. Galvin Pkwy.
Best Time to Visit:	Spring, fall, winter; early morning is best during the summer
Visitor Center/Museum:	Yes
Hours:	May-Labor Day 7:30 a.m.-4 p.m.; Labor Day-April 9 a.m.-5 p.m.; call regarding hours for special programs
Fee Area:	Yes; 13-59 $8.50; 60 & up $7.50; 3-12 $4.25; under 3 free
Restroom:	Yes; barrier free
Wheelchair/Stroller Access:	Yes; chairs & strollers available for rent - chairs $5, strollers from $2-$8
Drinking Water:	Yes
Picnic Area:	Yes
Lodging:	No
Camping:	No; Zoo Night Camp is exception
Suitable for:	All ages
Notes/Tips:	The Phoenix Zoo offers other exciting programs not listed here; call for details & schedule

Internationally renowned for achieving astounding success breeding and re-introducing rare and endangered animals to the wild, the Phoenix Zoo is also recognized as one of the finest metropolitan zoos in the country. It's also a heck-of-a-lot of fun.

Easy, paved walking trails wind through the 125-acre park, connecting a number of different habitats, including an African savanna, Sonoran desert, rain forest and inland swamp. The remarkable Forest of Uco, a high-mountain rain forest, features the very rare South American spectacled bear.

In December, the zoo hosts the immensely popular "Zoo Lights" holiday festival. From the glow of almost a million lights, visitors can stroll the grounds after dark. During the summer months, the "Zoo Night Camp" gives kids and their parents the unique opportunity to enjoy a sleep over, discover nocturnal animals that are seldom seen and take a sunrise behind-the-scenes tour.

Phoenix Zoo, 455 N. Galvin Pkwy., Phoenix, AZ 85008, 602-273-1341

7 Desert Botanical Garden

Location:	On N. Galvin Pkwy. in Papago Park
Best Time to Visit:	Early spring, fall, winter
Visitor Center/Museum:	Yes
Hours:	Daily 7 a.m.-8 p.m.; closed Christmas
Fee Area:	Yes; 12 & up $7.50; 60 & up $6.50; 5-12 $1.50; under 5 free
Restroom:	Yes; barrier free
Wheelchair/Stroller Access:	Yes; 2 chairs available for rent on first-come basis, $2
Drinking Water:	Yes
Picnic Area:	No; patio cafe open from 8 a.m.-2 p.m.
Lodging:	No
Camping:	No
Suitable for:	All ages

Also located in Papago Park, just north of the Phoenix Zoo, you'll discover one of the finest botanical gardens in the Southwest. At 150 acres, it takes awhile to see all of the Desert Botanical Garden, but it's worth the effort.

A short hike along the splendid "Plants and People of the Sonoran Desert" loop trail is beautiful and educational. You'll learn how people, plants and animals have learned to survive in the Sonoran desert. An entertaining interactive program called "Desert Detectives" is a self-guided tour game designed for kids. You may pickup some energy and water conservation tips when visiting the futuristic Desert House. Wonderful holiday programs are also very popular.

Desert Botanical Garden, 1201 N. Galvin Pkwy., Phoenix, AZ 85008, 602-941-1225

8 Heritage Square

Location:	Park entrance & exit is on 6th St., just south of Monroe
Best Time to Visit:	Anytime
Visitor Center/Museum:	Yes
Hours:	Wed.-Sat. 10 a.m.-4 p.m.; Sun. noon-4 p.m.
Fee Area:	Yes; for tours of the Rosson House; 12 & up $3; under 12 $1
Restroom:	Yes; barrier free
Wheelchair/Stroller Access:	Limited to grounds & first floors of houses. Rosson House has a chair lift that circumvents the entry stairs
Drinking Water:	Yes
Picnic Area:	No tables; picnicking allowed on lawn
Lodging:	No
Camping:	No
Suitable For:	All ages; best appreciated by kids studying Arizona history

On a block dating from the 1800s, Heritage Square is a striking remnant of the city's Victorian past. Museums, shops and restaurants now inhabit the block, but the main attraction are the five marvelous old homes that are the only remaining resident structures of the original Phoenix townsite.

The cornerstone of Heritage Square is the Rosson House, built in 1895 by a doctor who was elected mayor. I recommend taking the 30-minute guided tour of this remarkable mansion. Afterward, enjoy a variety of authentic Victorian pastries, sandwiches and other treats at the Teeter House tearoom. You can dine indoors, but I suggest putting a blanket on the lawn and have an old-fashioned picnic.

Heritage Square is part of Heritage and Science Park which includes the Arizona Science Center and Phoenix Museum of History.

Heritage Square, 600 E. Adams St., Phoenix, AZ 85004, 602-262-5071 or 602-262-5029 (recorded information)

9 **Arizona Science Center**

Location:	On Washington St. @ Heritage Square Park
Best Time to Visit:	Anytime
Visitor Center/Museum:	Yes
Hours:	Daily 8 a.m-5 p.m.; closed Thanksgiving & Christmas
Fee Area:	Yes; exhibits only: $6-$8; exhibits & planetarium or film: $8-$10; exhibits, planetarium & film: $9-$11
Restroom:	Yes; barrier free
Wheelchair/Stroller Access:	Yes; entire center
Drinking Water:	Yes
Suitable for:	All ages

A first-rate family experience, the 120,000-square-foot Arizona Science Center is one of the "Points of Pride" of Phoenix.

"Hands on" is the order of the day at the Science Center. The fascinating exhibits are entertaining and educational for folks of all ages. Don't miss the planetarium or the impressive IWERKS theater. Under the doom of planetarium, you can take a magical, three-dimensional flight through the solar system. The 50-foot IWERKS theater features astounding films about natural science, earth science and space science.

Arizona Science Center, 600 E. Washington St., Phoenix, AZ 85004, 602-716-2000

Phoenix Museum of History

10

Location:	On 5th St. @ Heritage Square Park
Best Time to Visit:	Anytime
Visitor Center/Museum:	Yes
Hours:	Mon.-Sat 10 a.m.-5 p.m.; Sun. noon-5 p.m. Open all holidays
Fee Area:	Yes; 12 & up $5; 7-11 $2.50; under 7 free
Restroom:	Yes; barrier free
Wheelchair/Stroller Access:	Yes; entire museum
Drinking Water:	Yes
Suitable for:	All ages

I first experienced the Phoenix Museum of History on a field trip with my daughter Merritt's 4th grade class. But this remarkable museum rates repeat visits.

You'll discover interactive exhibits that, in an entertaining way, introduce guests to the history of Phoenix, from pre-Columbian times to the present. The old photographs, books and records will be a hit with adults. Kids can pack a wagon, pretending they are preparing for a cross-country wagon train adventure.

Phoenix Museum of History, 105 N. 5th St., Phoenix, AZ 85004, 602-253-2734

Arizona Mining & Mineral Museum

11

Location:	On West Washington St. in downtown Phoenix
Best Time to Visit:	Anytime
Visitor Center/Museum:	Yes
Hours:	Mon.-Fri. 8 a.m.-5 p.m.; Sat. 11 a.m.-4 p.m.; closed Sun & State holidays
Fee Area:	No
Restroom:	Yes; barrier free

Wheelchair/Stroller Access:	Yes
Drinking Water:	Yes
Suitable for:	All ages

Highlighting Arizona's colorful and historic mining tradition, the Arizona Mining & Mineral Museum is anything but dull. There are over 3,000 minerals on exhibit including an eight-foot piece of native copper, a large quartz geode—each half weighing 240 pounds, rocks from the first Moon landing, and a fragment of Meteor Crater's meteorite weighing 206 pounds.

Kids will appreciate the many hands-on experiments. The museum also hosts rock hounding and prospecting field trips for all ages.

Arizona Mining & Mineral Museum, 1502 W. Washington St., Phoenix, AZ 85007, 602-255-3795

12 Heard Museum

Location:	On E. Monte Vista Rd. in central Phoenix
Best Time to Visit:	Anytime
Visitor Center/Museum:	Yes
Hours:	Daily 9:30 a.m.-5 p.m.; closed major holidays
Fee Area:	Yes; 12 & up $7; 65 & up $6; 4-12 $3; under 4 free
Restroom:	Yes; barrier free
Wheelchair/Stroller Access:	Yes; entire facility
Drinking Water:	Yes
Picnic Area:	No; Ironwood Cafe is open daily
Suitable for:	All ages

Going away, the Heard is the finest museum in the country featuring Native American culture, history and art.

In the expansive 10 galleries, you'll discover an astounding collection of Hopi kachina dolls, the remarkable Barry Goldwater photograph exhibit, exceptional examples of weaving, pottery, bead work, fine art and Navajo rugs.

This very special museum also features multi-media presentations, an annual Native American Arts and Crafts Show and hands-on activities for kids. I recommend visiting the Heard during the Dia de los Muertos (Day of the Dead) weekend celebration, usually held over a weekend in October. Very educational and great fun. The Heard Museum is a must see.

Heard Museum, 22 E. Monte Vista Rd., Phoenix, Az 85004, 602-252-8840

13 Phoenix Art Museum

Location:	On North Central Ave. in downtown Phoenix
Best Time to Visit:	Anytime
Visitor Center/Museum:	Yes
Hours:	Tues. & Weds., Fri-Sun. 10 a.m.-5 p.m.; Thurs. 10 a.m.-9 p.m. Closed Mon. and all major holidays
Fee Area:	Yes; adults $7; seniors & full-time citizens $5; ages 6-17 $2; free for museum members and kids under 6; free to everyone on Thursday. Call for admission prices to traveling/limited engagement programs.
Restroom:	Yes
Wheelchair/Stroller Access:	Yes
Drinking Water:	Yes
Suitable for:	All ages

Founded in 1949 and opened in 1959, the Phoenix Art Museum recently completed a $25 million expansion and renovation. With a whopping 160,000 square feet, the remarkable museum is one of the largest visual arts institutions in the Southwest. The 16,000 works on display span the centuries and emphasize American Arts; European Art of the 14th-19th Centuries; Western American Art; Modern & Contemporary Art; Spanish & Latin American Art; 18th-20th Century Fashion Design; and the Throne Miniature Rooms.

Besides hosting many traveling exhibits (including Treasures of Egypt), the museum features an interactive "child friendly, please touch!" gallery called ArtWorks.

Phoenix Art Museum, 1625 N. Central Ave., Phoenix, Az 85004, 602-257-1222

The Phoenix
14 Mountain Preserves

Location:	With the exception of Thunderbird on 59th Ave., and Papago on Galvin Pkwy., the preserves are situated between Camelback & Bell Rds (south to north) and I-17 & Scottsdale Rd. (west to east)
Best Time to Visit:	Early spring, fall, winter
Visitor Center/Museum:	No
Hours:	Varies; call for specifics
Fee Area:	No
Restrooms:	Yes; at most picnic sites and near many trailheads. No facilities along trails
Wheelchair/Stroller Access:	Limited mostly to picnic grounds
Drinking Water:	Yes; at picnic areas and some trailheads; see Notes/Tips
Picnic Area:	At most parks; call for details & reservations if needed
Lodging:	No
Camping:	No
Suitable for:	Picnicking & short hikes for all ages; many trails best for experienced hikers
Notes/Tips:	When hiking, mountain biking or horseback riding, always take at least a quart of water per person, more is better. Know and obey trail right-of-way rules. Avoid rattlesnake encounters by staying on established trails and don't step or reach where you can't see. To preserve the beauty of the parks, don't be a trailblazer.
The Preserves:	Camelback/Echo Canyon Park, Papago Park, Lookout Mountain, North Mountain, Shaw Butte, Shadow Mountain, Squaw Peak, Stony/Echo Mountain, Thunderbird Recreation Area

Phoenicians are justifiably proud and protective of their metropolitan mountains. Phoenix boasts the best urban and near-urban hiking, mountain biking and equestrian parks of any large city.

Within city limits, you'll find nine unique mountains that offer a variety of desert trails that range from easy to very challenging. Everyday, even in the hottest part of the summer, thousands of outdoor enthusiasts converge on the mountain preserves. In fact, the Summit Trail on Squaw Peak is the most hiked trail in the United States. Below are the names of these wonderful mountain preserves. However, a description of each is beyond the scope of this book. For detailed information, including excellent trail maps, I suggest *Day Hikes and Trail Rides in and Around Phoenix* authored by Roger and Ethel Freeman

For information & maps: Phoenix Parks, Recreation & Library Dept., 2333 N. Central Ave., Phoenix, AZ 85009, 602-272-8871
or
Phoenix Mountains Preservation Council, P.O. Box 26121, Phoenix, AZ 85068-6121, 602-265-8397

Deer Valley Rock Art Center

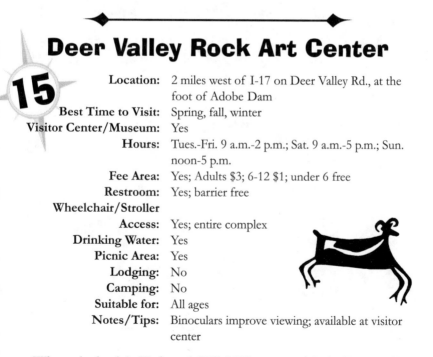

Location:	2 miles west of I-17 on Deer Valley Rd., at the foot of Adobe Dam
Best Time to Visit:	Spring, fall, winter
Visitor Center/Museum:	Yes
Hours:	Tues.-Fri. 9 a.m.-2 p.m.; Sat. 9 a.m.-5 p.m.; Sun. noon-5 p.m.
Fee Area:	Yes; Adults $3; 6-12 $1; under 6 free
Restroom:	Yes; barrier free
Wheelchair/Stroller Access:	Yes; entire complex
Drinking Water:	Yes
Picnic Area:	Yes
Lodging:	No
Camping:	No
Suitable for:	All ages
Notes/Tips:	Binoculars improve viewing; available at visitor center

Where the heck is Hedgpeth Hills? When you visit the Deer Valley Rock Art Center, you'll be standing at Hedgpeth.

Concentrated on the lower slopes of Hedgpeth Hills in northwest Phoenix is the largest petroglyph site in the Phoenix Metropolitan area. At this 47-acre natural desert preserve where native plants and animals are protected, you'll find an impressive interpretive museum, petroglyph viewing from a gently sloping, barrier-free, quarter-mile path and interactive displays.

The remarkable visitor center appears as if it grew out of the hill. Here, you'll learn about the 1,500 rock cravings and the culture that pecked the designs more than 1,000 years ago. Kids programs included re-producing petroglyph images on cardboard.

Deer Valley Rock Art Center, 3711 W. Deer Valley Rd., Phoenix, AZ 85080, 602-582-8007

16 Luke Air Force Base

Location:	Main entrance to the base is at the intersection of Litchfield Rd. & Glendale Ave. in Litchfield Park (far west Valley)
Best Time to Visit:	Spring, fall, winter
Visitor Center/Museum:	Yes
Hours:	Tours arranged Mon.-Fri., at 9 a.m.*
Fee Area:	No
Restroom:	Yes; barrier free
Wheelchair/Stroller Access:	Yes; advise of requirements when making reservations
Drinking Water:	Yes; but bring water bottles
Picnic Area:	Yes; in base parks
Lodging:	No
Camping:	No
Suitable for:	Best for ages 6 & up; noise will be too much for young children

Ah, the magnificent sound of freedom. You will hear it's deafening roar when you visit Luke Air Force Base.

A tour of Luke Air Force Base is a surefire way to get a huge jolt of adrenaline and to experience that wonderful swelling in your chest called patriotism.

First stop is at the 506th Support Center building for a audio/ visual presentation hosted by an Air Force officer. Afterward, you'll board a bus for a narrated tour of the huge base with a final stop on the flight line.

Standing on the tarmac, you'll see, here and feel the awesome power of F-16 fighter jets when the pilots ignite afterburners for take off. After landing, the jets will taxi less than a 100 feet from your position. Kids will appreciate the friendly smiles and waves from the pilots.

This is a high-charged adventure and an rewarding educational experience.

*Note: Since the terrorist attacks of 9/11/01, tours have been limited to established groups until further notice. Contact the Public Affairs office for details.

Luke Air Force Base, 13960 Eagle St., Litchfield Park, AZ 85309, 623-856-5853 (Public Affairs)

17 Lake Pleasant Desert Center

Location:	At Lake Pleasant; on 87th Ave. in Peoria
Best Time to Visit:	Early spring, fall, winter
Visitor Center/Museum:	Yes
Hours:	Varies by season & program; call for details
Fee Area:	Yes; varies by program and desired amenities
Restroom:	Yes; barrier free
Wheelchair/Stroller Access:	Yes
Drinking Water:	Yes
Picnic Area:	Yes
Lodging:	No
Camping:	Yes; at Lake Pleasant
Suitable for:	All ages
Notes/Tips:	Reservations are required. Call for requirements regarding minimum and maximum group sizes.

The Desert Outdoor Center has been described as an "educator's dream" complete with science lab, computer room, and Internet access. The facility also features a resource room, a lecture room, kitchen, a large multi-purpose room, and an amphitheater, and dormitories that can sleep up to 100 people.

This remarkable desert-learning center is a resource for limitless learning and research. The Center offers programs for half-day, full-day, and overnight visits..

Desert Outdoor Center at Lake Pleasant, 41402 N. 87th Ave., Peoria, AZ 85383, 928-501-1730

White Tank Mountain Regional Park

18

Location:	Only one access point: Olive Ave. (extension of Dunlap) ends at park entrance.
Best Time to Visit:	Early spring, fall, winter
Visitor Center/Museum:	No; ranger booth only
Hours:	Park gate: Sun.-Thur. 6 a.m.-8 p.m.; Fri.-Sat. 6 a.m.-10 p.m.; overnight campers are locked in
Fee Area:	Yes; Day use $3 per vehicle; camping w/water & power $15 per night
Restroom:	Yes; barrier free
Wheelchair/Stroller Access:	Yes; all campgrounds and portions of some trails
Drinking Water:	Yes; see Notes/Tips
Picnic Area:	Yes; family & group sites; many with ramadas
Lodging:	No
Camping:	Yes; family & group sites with restrooms, water. power
Suitable for:	All ages
Notes/Tips:	When hiking, carry plenty of water, wear hats, sunglasses and hiking boots. This rattlesnake country so stay on trails & give snakes right-of-way

Outstanding hiking, horseback riding, camping, wildlife observation and petroglyph viewing are offered at White Tank Mountain Regional Park in western Maricopa County.

This stunning desert preserve features a number of challenging hiking trails. The Waterfall Trail, however, is short, easy and suitable for the entire family.

Located adjacent to a picnic/camping site and kid's playground, the trail begins as a level, wide dirt path that will accommodate chairs and strollers. On the right, near the half-mile mark, you'll spot a number of petroglyphs carved by the Hohokam a 1,000 years ago. At this point the trail becomes rocky and impassable for chairs. The trail winds through a narrow canyon, ending at the back of the gorge. If there have been recent rains, you'll see a waterfall, hence the name.

If you aren't experienced desert hikers or campers, I recommend the park and this hike.

White Tank Mountain Regional Park, P.O. Box 91, Waddell, AZ 85355, 623-935-2505

19 Challenger Learning Center of Arizona

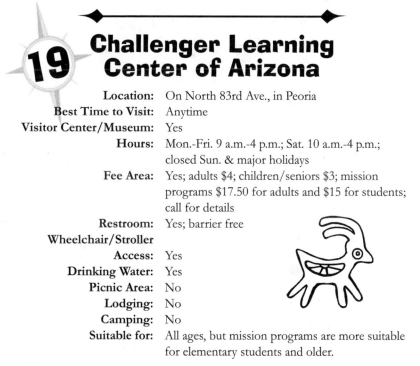

Location:	On North 83rd Ave., in Peoria
Best Time to Visit:	Anytime
Visitor Center/Museum:	Yes
Hours:	Mon.-Fri. 9 a.m.-4 p.m.; Sat. 10 a.m.-4 p.m.; closed Sun. & major holidays
Fee Area:	Yes; adults $4; children/seniors $3; mission programs $17.50 for adults and $15 for students; call for details
Restroom:	Yes; barrier free
Wheelchair/Stroller Access:	Yes
Drinking Water:	Yes
Picnic Area:	No
Lodging:	No
Camping:	No
Suitable for:	All ages, but mission programs are more suitable for elementary students and older.

With now a network of over 40 centers spanning across the country, as well as in Great Britain and Canada, Peoria is the proud home of the Knight Space Science Education Center and the Challenger Learning Center of Arizona.

Named for the Challenger Space Shuttle that was tragically destroyed during launch, this wonderful center should be on your "must visit" list. Here, you'll discover the wonders of the universe with numerous hands-on, interactive exhibits and experiments. But the real treat at the Challenger Center is the opportunity to participate in a Shuttle Mission. Whether you are a member of the mission control ground team, or an astronaut aboard the shuttle, this experience is exciting, educational, and a whole lot of fun. Do it!.

Challenger Learning Center of Arizona, 21170 N. 83rd Ave., Peoria, AZ 85382, 623-322-2001

◆━━━━━━━━━━━━━━━━━━━━◆

20 Pioneer Arizona Living History Museum

Location:	Off I-17 on Pioneer Rd. (exit 225), 25 mi. No. of Phoenix
Best Time to Visit:	Early spring, fall, winter
Visitor Center/Museum:	Yes
Hours:	Wed.-Sun. 9 a.m-5 p.m.; guided tours 10 a.m.-1 p.m.
Fee Area:	Yes; self-guided discovery $3; guided tour $6
Restroom:	Yes; barrier free
Wheelchair/Stroller Access:	Yes
Drinking Water:	Yes
Picnic Area:	Yes
Lodging:	No
Camping:	No
Suitable for:	All ages

Referring to this marvelous facility as a museum or western theme park is a big stretch. The Pioneer Arizona Living History Museum is really a community that includes 28 original and reconstructed buildings that were brought in from all over Arizona. The emphasis is on education and authenticity.

You'll find a genuine 19th century schoolhouse, blacksmith shop with a working smith and a print shop. You can walk the streets of this unique reminder of Arizona's rough 'n' tumble territorial days. I suggest taking a guided tour. The guides, dressed in period costume, offer fascinating insights about Arizona's wild west past.

Pioneer Arizona Living History Museum, 3901 W. Pioneer Rd., Phoenix, AZ 85027, 623-465-1052

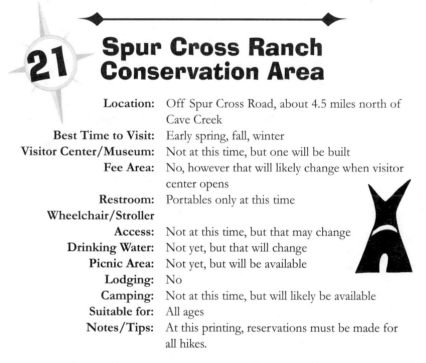

21 Spur Cross Ranch Conservation Area

Location:	Off Spur Cross Road, about 4.5 miles north of Cave Creek
Best Time to Visit:	Early spring, fall, winter
Visitor Center/Museum:	Not at this time, but one will be built
Fee Area:	No, however that will likely change when visitor center opens
Restroom:	Portables only at this time
Wheelchair/Stroller Access:	Not at this time, but that may change
Drinking Water:	Not yet, but that will change
Picnic Area:	Not yet, but will be available
Lodging:	No
Camping:	Not at this time, but will likely be available
Suitable for:	All ages
Notes/Tips:	At this printing, reservations must be made for all hikes.

Historic Spur Cross Ranch that encompasses some of the most pristine Sonoran desert landscape is now a new Maricopa County Park. Although limited at this printing to guided hikes, plans include construction of a visitor center and hiking trails. This magnificent park also features a number of archaeological sites including the ruins of Hohokam villages and fine examples of ancient petroglyphs. The park also protects the last remaining perennial spring in Arizona.

Spur Cross Ranch Conservation Area, 37622 N. Cave Creek Rd., Cave Creek, AZ 85331, 623-480-1400

Mistress Mine

Location:	North of Carefree off Seven Springs Rd. (Forest Service 24); entrance is 1.5 miles after pavement ends
Best Time to Visit:	Early spring, fall, winter
Visitor Center/Museum:	Yes; with gift shop
Hours:	Daily 10 a.m.-5 p.m.; hours may vary during July & Aug.
Fee Area:	No entrance fee; $3 for guided tour
Restroom:	Yes; difficult, but possible for chairs
Wheelchair/Stroller Access:	Limited; ground level only
Drinking Water:	Yes; but suggest bringing water bottles
Picnic Area:	Yes; under shade trees
Lodging:	Yes; a very large teepee that passes for a very rustic B&B; for adults that like roughing it-not for most kids
Camping:	No; Seven Springs campground is about 7 miles north of mine
Suitable for:	All ages

Located in the Tonto Forest on Seven Springs Road, the Cave Creek Mistress Mine was a profitable gold mine in the late 1800s. Today, this fascinating mining camp is a "must see" for Arizona history buffs, rock hounds, amateur geologists and kids who just like to collect rocks.

Hundreds of trays of rocks and minerals are displayed along the elevated boardwalk leading to the gift shop and mine entrance. A tour of the operation begins at the back of the gift shop, where a narrow tunnel leads to the mine shaft. Director Ron Kaczor conducts the very informative narrated tour.

This is also a great place to see desert wildlife, including a not-so-wild burro named Gabby, that Kaczor has taught to "grin" for the photographs you'll want to take.

Cave Creek Mistress Mine, P.O. Box 5754, Carefree, AZ 85377, 480-488-0842

23 McCormick-Stillman Railroad Park

Location:	On Indian Bend Road in Scottsdale
Best Time to Visit:	Early spring, fall, winter
Visitor Center/Museum:	Yes
Hours:	Seasonal; call for details
Fee Area:	There is no admission for entering the park. Train and carousel rides are $1 per rider; kids under age 3 ride free with paying adult
Restroom:	Yes; barrier free
Wheelchair/Stroller Access:	Yes
Drinking Water:	Yes
Picnic Area:	Yes; many tables with shade
Lodging:	No
Camping:	No
Suitable for:	All ages

Encompassing 30 acres, McCormick-Stillman Railroad Park is a must do for train buffs and families who just want to have fun. Kids will delight in riding the miniature train and very special carousel. The 1928 Roald Amundsen Pullman car and model train displays are a hit with adults and kids alike. There are a number of shaded ramadas with picnic tables and charcoal grills for your family outing.

McCormick-Stillman Railroad Park, 7301 E. Indian Bend Rd., Scottsdale, AZ 85250, 480-312-2312

Out of Africa Wildlife Park

24

Location:	On Fort McDowell Rd., 2 miles miles north of Shea Blvd. off Beeline Hwy. (AZ 87)
Best Time to Visit:	Early spring, fall, winter
Visitor Center/Museum:	No; up-scale mercantile & gift shop
Hours:	Labor Day-Memorial Day wknd., Tues.-Sun. 9:30 a.m.-5 p.m.; June-Aug., Wed.-Sun. 9:30 a.m.-5 p.m.; Memorial Day wknd-Sept. Sat. evening dinner & show 9:300 a.m.-9:30 p.m.; closed Thanksgiving & Christmas
Fee Area:	Yes; varies by season & current programs; call in advance
Restroom:	Yes; barrier free
Wheelchair/Stroller Access:	Yes; entire facility. Chair & stroller rentals available
Drinking Water:	Yes
Picnic Area:	Yes
Lodging:	No
Camping:	No
Suitable for:	All ages
Notes/Tips:	Kalahari Cafe offers good food at reasonable prices

Out of Africa Wildlife Park is not a zoo, circus or drive-through animal viewing park. Here, the focus is on big, wild animals that actually live with the staff.

Out of Africa features large bears, tigers, lions and even wolves. The animals frolic with themselves and their handlers on land and in large pools. These animal/human interactions are not rehearsed shows; everything is spontaneous. I think you'll be particularly impressed watching huge carnivores featured in a program called "Tiger Splash."

Out of Africa Wildlife Animal Park, #2 Ft. McDowell Rd., P.O. Box 17928, Fountain Hills, AZ 85269, 480-837-7779

Mesa Southwest Museum

25

Location:	On North MacDonald Drive in Mesa
Best Time to Visit:	Anytime
Visitor Center/Museum:	Yes
Hours:	Tues.-Sat. 10 a.m.-5 p.m.; Sun. 1 p.m.-5 p.m.
Fee Area:	Yes; adults $6; seniors & students $5; ages 3-12 $3; under 3 free
Restroom:	Yes; barrier free
Wheelchair/Stroller Access:	Yes
Drinking Water:	Yes
Picnic Area:	No
Lodging:	No
Camping:	No
Suitable for:	All ages

Arizona's natural history museum explores Southwestern history from the time of the dinosaurs to the present. The Prehistoric Wing allows visitors to explore Dinosaur Mountain and the underwater world of Arizona's prehistoric oceans. The Discovery Resource Center is a kid's hands-on experience featuring interactive computer games to dinosaur bones and art material. Through artifacts, petroglyphs and fascinating exhibits, learn about Arizona's native people, from Paleo-Indians to today's Apache and Pima tribes.

This museum should be on your must see list.

Mesa Southwest Museum, 53 N. MacDonald, Mesa, AZ 85201, 480-644-2230

Taliesin West

26

Location:	On north Frank Lloyd Wright Blvd. in Scottsdale
Best Time to Visit:	Anytime
Visitor Center/Museum:	Yes
Hours:	Tours offered daily; call for times

Fee Area:	Basic tours; adults $16; seniors & students $14; ages 4-12 $3; under 4 free. Other tour prices vary
Restroom:	Yes; barrier free
Wheelchair/Stroller Access:	Yes
Drinking Water:	Yes
Picnic Area:	No
Lodging:	No
Camping:	No
Suitable for:	All ages

Opened in 1937, Taliesin West served as the winter home of renowned architect Frank Lloyd Wright. Although Wright died in 1959, Taliesin West is an ongoing project, constantly being revised and improved. Tours of this fascinating home/school vary from a 60-minute "Panorama Tour" or a 90-minute "Insight Tour" to a three-hour "Behind the Scenes Tour." Also available seasonally are the 90-minute "Desert Walk," which explores the desert trails around the complex, and the two-hour "Apprentice Shelter Tour," an apprentice-guided discovery of the desert shelters built by students at Taliesin West.

Taliesin West, 12621 N. Frank Lloyd Wright Blvd., Scottsdale, AZ 85261, 480-860-2700

27 Salt River Tubing and Recreation

Location:	Salt River HQ is on Power Rd. in N.E. Mesa, 15 miles north of U.S. 60
Best Time to Visit:	Summer
Visitor Center/Museum:	No; headquarters has a gift and mini market
Hours:	May-Sept. daily beginning @ 9 a.m.
Fee Area:	Yes; $9 per person. Group rates available
Restroom:	Yes

Wheelchair/Stroller Access:	No
Drinking Water:	At headquarters; bring plenty of water
Picnic Area:	No
Lodging:	No
Camping:	No
Suitable for:	Kids must be 8 years or older and/or 48" tall. Life jackets are recommended, but not provided. Wear old sneakers or river boots, hats, sunblock and sunglasses. AVOID TOO MUCH SUN EXPOSURE; I recommend lycra suits, or light weight, full-body cover-up. Ask for a brochure that includes a river floating checklist

On summer weekends, many desert dwellers beat the heat on the cool and refreshing waters of the Salt River. Salt River Tubing and Recreation offers innertube float trips ranging from one to five miles.

You begin your tubing adventure at the Salt River Headquarters. The company provides shuttle and bus service from different parking lots in the Salt River Recreation area. Sturdy river tubes are provided. Rental tubes for ice chests are available.

Salt River Tubing & Recreation, P.O. Box 6568, Mesa, AZ 86216, 480-984-3305, FAX 480-984-0875, www.saltrivertubing.com

Southeastern Arizona Map

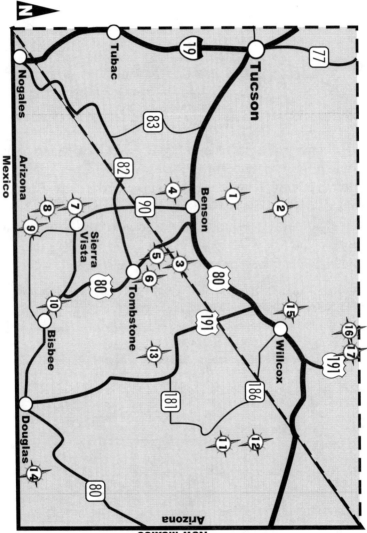

Chapter Five
Southeastern Arizona

Just after two in the afternoon on October 26, 1881, four angry men stood shoulder-to-shoulder in a vacant lot behind a horse stable. Concealed inside the duster worn by one man was a 10-gauge, short-barreled shotgun, commonly called a street howitzer. All were wearing sidearms, including another man's long-barreled Colt .44, dubbed the Peacemaker. Twenty feet separated the four men from five cowboys who were itching for a showdown.

In 27-seconds of blazing fury, about 30 shots were fired. The gunfight at the O.K. Corral in Tombstone became the most famous shootout in the colorful history of the Old West.

Southeastern Arizona is rich in history, legend and lore. Here, you can hike along the same trail used by the first Europeans when they entered present-day Arizona. In historic Bisbee, you'll don rain slickers and hard hats, climb aboard tiny railcars and descend 1,500 feet beneath a granite mountain. In a mystical mountain range you can explore the secret stronghold of legendary Apache Chief Cochise. You might want to spend a morning discovering the Fort Bowie National Historic Site and the afternoon at the Rex Allen Arizona Cowboy Museum in Willcox. If wilderness hiking and camping are your passion, plan an adventure in the magnificent Chiricahua Mountains. In the mountain community of Benson you can hop a train for a scenic ride along the banks of the San Pedro River, descend into a living cave and walk the dusty streets of a ghost town that really isn't.

East of Benson, huge boulders and stunning rock formations point the way to Texas Canyon and the headquarters of the Amerind Foundation. To the south, in the town "Too Tough to Die," you can stroll quietly through a hilltop graveyard, visit the saloons and gambling houses on Allen Street and put yourself at the O.K. Corral and imagine.

Benson

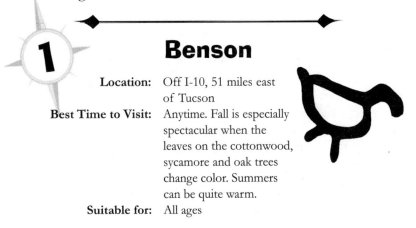

Location:	Off I-10, 51 miles east of Tucson
Best Time to Visit:	Anytime. Fall is especially spectacular when the leaves on the cottonwood, sycamore and oak trees change color. Summers can be quite warm.
Suitable for:	All ages

With the opening of Karchner Caverns State Park, the small community of Benson is experiencing an economic revival. Because of the dramatic increase in tourism, existing motels and restaurants have been spruced-up and new establishments are under construction.

Still, Benson is a quiet, restful town and the gateway to many of the attractions in southeastern Arizona. For information regarding lodging and services, contact the Benson-San Pedro Valley Chamber of Commerce.

Benson-San Pedro Valley Chamber of Commerce, 363 W. 4th Street, Box 2255, Benson, AZ 85520, 520-586-2842

Gammon's Gulch Ghost Town

2

Location:	Go one mile east of Benson on I-10. Exit at Pomerene/Cascabel Rd., exit 306. Go about 12 miles, or until the pavement ends. Go one mile and turn left on a dirt road that is marked with the Gammon's Gulch sign.
Best Time to Visit:	Anytime; winters can be chilly; summers are warm
Visitor Center/Museum:	The entire town is a museum
Hours:	Daily during daylight hours, but advanced notice is appreciated
Fee Area:	Yes; $5 per person; $4 for seniors
Restrooms:	Yes; but out-house style
Wheelchair/Stroller Access:	Streets and boardwalks only; buildings and the restroom aren't barrier-free.
Drinking Water:	Yes; but take water bottles
Picnic Area:	Yes
Lodging:	Yes; charming but rustic bed-and-breakfast accommodations best suited for adventurous adults, not families. Reservations required. $35 to $45 per night.
Camping:	No
Suitable for:	All ages, remembering that services are very limited.
Notes/Tips:	This is rattlesnake country so stay on trails. Warm clothing and jackets are recommended in fall and winter.

Jay Gammon, a former Hollywood set designer who specialized in building backdrops for western films, just had to have his own ghost town. When he couldn't find a town to purchase, Gammon built his own.

Tucked away in a secluded canyon, Gammon's Gulch Ghost Town may not be authentic, but it could be. All of the material used in the construction, right down to most of the nails, was taken from genuine ghost towns that were being demolished. Even the ore cars and tools used to dig the make believe gold mine are the real thing. The thousands of artifacts dating from the early 1800s are in working condition. Many of the props that Gammon has collected over the years were used in western films, including *Tombstone* and Kevin Costner's *Wyatt Earp*.

Gammon's Gulch, P.O. Box 76, Pomerene, AZ 85627, 520-212-2831, e-mail: gammonsgulch@theriver.com, www.gammonsgulch.com

3 Amerind Foundation

Location:	12 miles east of Benson off I-10. Take Dragoon Rd (exit 318) one mile to the foundation
Best Time to Visit:	Spring, fall
Visitor Center/Museum:	Yes
Hours:	Sept. - May, daily 10 a.m.-4 p.m.; June - Aug., Wed.-Sun. 10 a.m.-4 p.m.; closed New Years, Easter, July 4, Thanksgiving, Christmas
Fee Area:	Yes; adults $3; 60 and above $2; 12-18 $2; under 12 free
Restroom:	Yes
Wheelchair/Stroller Access:	No
Drinking Water:	Yes
Picnic Area:	Yes; with shaded ramadas
Lodging:	No
Camping:	No
Suitable for:	All ages

In 1937, William Fulton, an amateur archaeologist and Native American historian, was so taken by the beauty of Texas Canyon in the rugged Dragoon Mountains, he founded Amerind Foundation to further research and encourage understanding of Indian cultures.

Surrounded by towering rock formations, the museum/research center includes wonderful archaeological exhibits, priceless photographs and Native American craftwork. Visiting this splendid foundation is not only delightful from a scenery stand point, but very educational, especially for kids.

Amerind Foundation, P.O. Box 400, Dragoon, AZ 85609, 520-586-4679, www.amerind.org

Kartchner Caverns State Park

4

Location:	9 miles south of I-10 at the Sierra Vista/Fort Huachua exit 302; about 12 miles west & south of Benson
Best Time to Visit:	Anytime
Visitor Center/Museum:	Yes; with theaters, interactive exhibits, kids activities, including programs for the visually impaired
Hours:	Daily from 8 a.m.-6 p.m.; cave tours from 8:30 a.m.-4:30 p.m. Closed at 2 p.m. on Thanksgiving & Christmas Eve; closed Christmas Day
Fee Area:	Yes; $11 per carload into the park, Discovery Center, exhibit complex, picnic area, hiking & hummingbird garden. Cave tours, adults, $13; 7-13, $5; under 6, free. Camping, $17 per site
Restroom:	Yes; barrier-free
Wheelchair/Stroller Access:	Yes; interior cave trails are barrier-free with only a few areas of difficult grades that may require extra help. The entire concrete trail has hand rails and is 40 inches wide. The Discovery Center is ADA compliant with special seating, turn-around restrooms, phone, drinking fountains, signage and doors that meet ADA requirements.
Drinking Water:	Yes
Picnic Area:	Yes; shaded ramadas
Lodging:	No
Camping:	Yes; 63 sites
Suitable for:	All ages

Notes/Tips: Allow at least half-a-day for a very rewarding explore of Kartchner Caverns. Before your cave tour, you will instructed not to touch anything within the caverns. Doing so not only damages the delicate structures, it is also a criminal offense.

Superlatives cannot describe Kartchner Caverns. In my opinion, this living labyrinth is the crown jewel of the Arizona State Park System.

Prior to 1974, no humans had ever laid eyes on the wonders of this 2.5 mile, 99% humid cave just below the desert in the rugged Whetstone Mountains. In fact, when biologists first entered the caverns, they were stunned upon discovering at least eight species previously unknown to science.

A one-hour tour of the caverns will be the highlight of your visit. You will also find five miles of wonderful hiking trails, including a wheelchair/stroller accessible loop trail, a full-service campground, on-site interpretive programs, outdoor amphitheater and a world class Discovery Center.

Kartchner Caverns State Park is a **"must see."**

Kartchner Caverns State Park, P.O. Box 1849, Benson, AZ 85602, 520-586-4100, Internet/virtual tours: www.pr.state.az.us

5 Holy Trinity Monastery

Location:	In St. David on State Route 80
Best Time to Visit:	Anytime
Visitor Center/Museum:	Yes
Hours:	Varies; call for details
Fee Area:	No
Restroom:	Yes; barrier free
Wheelchair/Stroller Access:	Limited to Monastery grounds and some buildings. Nature trail is not accessible.
Drinking Water:	Yes
Picnic Area:	Yes
Lodging:	Yes
Camping:	Limited to self-contained RVs and trailers
Suitable for:	All ages
Notes/Tips:	Reservations are required for meals with the residents or overnight stays. The nature trail passes through sections of a cemetery; be respectful

Located between Benson and Tombstone, this Benectine religious community features a 130-acre bird sanctuary along the San Pedro River. The dense riverside forest, thick stands of cedars, and small pond draw a variety of birds, making the Monastery one of the best bird watching locations in Arizona. The nature hike around the sanctuary is open to all visitors.

The monastery's museum features a different theme in each of its four rooms, including fascinating Nativity displays from around the world.

Holy Trinity Monastery, 520-720-4016

6 Tombstone

Location:	Off AZ 80, 25 miles south of Benson
Best Time to Visit:	Spring, fall, winter
Visitor Center/Museum:	Yes; at the Tombstone Courthouse State Historic Park
Hours:	Most attractions on Allen Street are open daily from 8 a.m.-9 p.m.; Courthouse State Park, daily from 8 a.m.-5 p.m.; closed Thanksgiving & Christmas
Fee Area:	Walking is free; you pay for everything else. Fees vary depending upon the sites visited; contact the Tombstone Office of Tourism
Restroom:	Yes; at the city park just north of the O.K. Corral and most establishments
Wheelchair/Stroller Access:	On the streets and boardwalks; most of the old buildings and historic sites are not entirely barrier free
Drinking Water:	Yes; at the city park and most establishments
Picnic Area:	Yes; at the Tombstone Courthosue State Historic Park
Lodging:	Yes; including the charming Best Western Look-Out Lodge and the beautifully restored 1880s Tombstone Boarding House, a bed-and-breakfast
Camping:	No
Suitable for:	All ages
Notes/Tips:	You won't find much shade, so wear hats, sunglasses and sunscreen. Bring water bottles. Food and beverages are available in many of the town's restored saloons. Bella Union and Nellie Cashman's are fine family restaurants.

In the late 1800s, the silver mining boom town of Tombstone was the biggest city between St. Louis and San Francisco. But it wasn't exactly cosmopolitan. Most of the business establishments on notorious Allen Street, the town's main drag, consisted of gambling halls, opium dens, houses of prostitution, saloons and outlaw hangouts.

At about the time the Earp brothers and John "Doc" Holiday shot it out with the McLaurys and Clantons at the O.K. Coral, the silver mines played out. Tombstone survived an earthquake and two fires, earning the nickname "The Town Too Tough To Die."

Today, unfortunately, Tombstone is an expensive tourist trap. Vendors sell everything from rubber tomahawks to buckskin shirts made in China. But if you look past the commercialism and keep a tight rein on your wallet, there are wonderful historic sights worth discovering.

I recommend visiting Boot Hill Graveyard, the Bird Cage Theater (where Wyatt Earp first met the lovely Josie Marcos), the Tombstone Courthouse State Historic Park, Fly Photography Exhibition Gallery and, of course, The O.K. Corral.

Best Western Look-Out Lodge, Box 787, Tombstone, AZ 85638, 520-457-2223

Tombstone Boarding House, 108 N. 4th St., Box 906, Tombstone, AZ 85638, 520-457-3716

Tombstone Office of Tourism, Box 917, Tombstone, AZ 85638, 520-457-3548 or 800-457-3423

---

7 Fort Huachuca

Location:	Off AZ 90, just west of downtown Sierra Vista
Best Time to Visit:	Anytime
Visitor Center/Museum:	Yes
Hours:	weekdays 9 a.m-4 p.m.; weekends 1 p.m.-4 p.m.
Fee Area:	No
Restroom:	Yes
Wheelchair/Stroller Access:	Yes
Drinking Water:	Yes
Picnic Area:	No
Lodging:	In Sierra Vista, not on the base
Camping:	No
Suitable for:	All ages

Headquarters for the United States Army's Global Information Systems Command, Fort Huachuca (wha-choo-ka) is the last of the territorial forts still in operation. Established in 1877, the historic part of the huge base is dedicated to preserving the heroic legacy of the Buffalo Soldiers, the first all-black regiment in the U.S. armed forces that battled renegade Apaches, Mexican bandits and American outlaws in the 1880s.

Fascinating Fort Huachuca Museum is housed in a 19th-century wooden building. The history of military life during territorial times is wonderfully highlighted.

Fort Huachuca, 520 538-7111

◆━━━━━━━━━━━━━━━━━━━━◆

Ramsey Canyon Preserve

8

Location:	Go about four miles south of Sierra Vista on AZ 90. Continue south on AZ 92 to the Ramsey Canyon Rd. Follow signs and continue for four miles.
Best Time to Visit:	Spring, summer, fall. At almost 6,000 ft., winters are cold
Visitor Center/Museum:	Yes
Hours:	Daily 8: a.m.-5 p.m. (see Notes/Tips)
Fee Area:	No; donations appreciated
Restrooms:	Yes; barrier-free
Wheelchair/Stroller Access:	Yes; at the visitor center only
Drinking Water:	Yes
Picnic Area:	Yes; but only a few tables
Lodging:	Yes; the preserve has six housekeeping cabins. Ramsey Canyon Inn, a terrific bed-and-breakfast, is adjacent to the preserve
Camping:	No
Suitable for:	All ages; best for kids and families with previous hiking experience
Notes/Tips:	Access and parking are purposely limited. Reservations are encouraged

Accessible only by hiking trails, this tiny nature preserve is recognized internationally as a wildlife and bird watching paradise. It is commonly called the "hummingbird capital of the world."

To help protect this delicate riparian ecosystem, the Nature Conservancy, owners of the site, place strict limits on the number of visitors that can enter the preserve at one time. Make advanced reservations. It will be worth your while.

Ramsey Canyon Inn, 520-378-3010
Ramsey Canyon Preserve, 27 Ramsey Canyon Rd., Hereford, AZ 85615, 520-378-2785

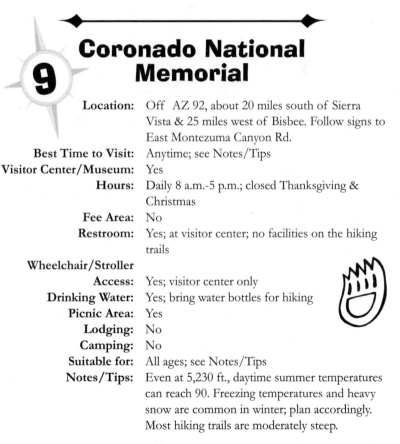

Coronado National Memorial

9

Location:	Off AZ 92, about 20 miles south of Sierra Vista & 25 miles west of Bisbee. Follow signs to East Montezuma Canyon Rd.
Best Time to Visit:	Anytime; see Notes/Tips
Visitor Center/Museum:	Yes
Hours:	Daily 8 a.m.-5 p.m.; closed Thanksgiving & Christmas
Fee Area:	No
Restroom:	Yes; at visitor center; no facilities on the hiking trails
Wheelchair/Stroller Access:	Yes; visitor center only
Drinking Water:	Yes; bring water bottles for hiking
Picnic Area:	Yes
Lodging:	No
Camping:	No
Suitable for:	All ages; see Notes/Tips
Notes/Tips:	Even at 5,230 ft., daytime summer temperatures can reach 90. Freezing temperatures and heavy snow are common in winter; plan accordingly. Most hiking trails are moderately steep.

Coronado National Memorial commemorates the first major European exploration of the American Southwest. It lies within an oak woodland in the scenic Huachuca Mountains through which the Francisco Vasquez de Coronado expedition entered present-day Arizona in search of the fabled Seven Cities of Cibola.

The memorial features a wonderful interpretative and cultural visitor center, miles of splendid hiking trails and, the impressive Coronado Cave.

Coronado National Memorial, 4101 E. Montezuma Canyon Road, Hereford, AZ 85615, 520-366-5515, www.nps.gov/coro.com

Bisbee

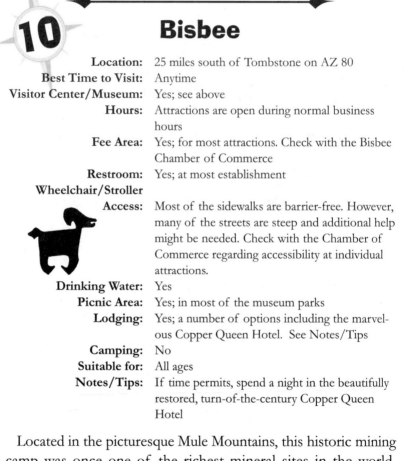

Location:	25 miles south of Tombstone on AZ 80
Best Time to Visit:	Anytime
Visitor Center/Museum:	Yes; see above
Hours:	Attractions are open during normal business hours
Fee Area:	Yes; for most attractions. Check with the Bisbee Chamber of Commerce
Restroom:	Yes; at most establishment
Wheelchair/Stroller Access:	Most of the sidewalks are barrier-free. However, many of the streets are steep and additional help might be needed. Check with the Chamber of Commerce regarding accessibility at individual attractions.
Drinking Water:	Yes
Picnic Area:	Yes; in most of the museum parks
Lodging:	Yes; a number of options including the marvelous Copper Queen Hotel. See Notes/Tips
Camping:	No
Suitable for:	All ages
Notes/Tips:	If time permits, spend a night in the beautifully restored, turn-of-the-century Copper Queen Hotel

Located in the picturesque Mule Mountains, this historic mining camp was once one of the richest mineral sites in the world, producing almost 3 million ounces of gold and a whooping 8 billion pounds of copper.

In the 1970s, when the price of copper nose-dived and the mines closed, the population began to shrink and Bisbee fell on hard times. But Bisbee has made a remarkable recovery. Today, Bisbee is a charming artist colony with an uncommon blend of romance, adventure and old west history.

When in Bisbee, be sure to take the Queen Mine Tour, a riding/walking trip down into the legendary Queen Mine. Visit historic Muheim House, an outstanding example of 19th century architecture and elegance, the Mining & Historical Museum or just stroll along the sidewalks and discover the many art galleries, coffee houses and Victorian homes.

Copper Queen Hotel, Drawer CQ, Bisbee, Az 85603, 520-432-2216 or 800-247-5829

Bisbee Chamber of Commerce, 7 Main St., Box BA, Bisbee, AZ 85603, 520-432-5421

11 Chiracahua National Monument

Location:	Off AZ 181, 60 miles north of Douglas
Ime to Visit:	Spring, fall; see Notes/Tips
Visitor Center/Museum:	Yes
Hours:	24 hr. access to the park. Visitor center daily 8 a.m.-5 p.m.; closed Christmas
Fee Area:	Day use $6; camping $8 per night
Restroom:	Yes; barrier-free
Wheelchair/Stroller Access:	Yes; at visitor center
Drinking Water:	Yes; at visitor center only
Picnic Area:	Yes
Lodging:	Not within park boundaries. Wonderful Chiricahua Foothills Bed & Breakfast is located 1/4-mile outside of the park; excellent home-cooked meals
Camping:	Yes
Suitable for:	All ages; see Notes/Tips

Notes/Tips: Mid-summer temperatures average 90. Heavy snowfall & below freezing temperatures are common in winter. Hiking in this rugged terrain requires careful planning & previous outdoor experience. When with kids, keep hikes short.

Called the "Land of the Standing-Up Rocks" by the Chiracahua (chair-a-cow-wa) Apache, this 12,000-acre park features strange rock pinnacles and spires, high desert and forest ecosystems and terrific hiking trails and camping sites. Considered a bird-watching mecca, these stunning mountains are also home to deer, mountain lions, javelina and the elusive coatimundi.

Park rangers at the visitor center give fascinating interpretive talks at the center's amphitheater.

Chiricahua National Monument, Dos Cabezas Route, Box 6500, Willcox, AZ 85643, 520-824-3560
Chiricahua Foothills Bed & Breakfast, 520-824-3632

Fort Bowie National Historical Site

12

Location:	Off AZ 181, about five miles north of Chiricahua National Monument. A well-maintained dirt road leads to the site
Best Time to Visit:	Spring, fall, early winter
Visitor Center/Museum:	Yes
Hours:	Daily 8 a.m.-5 p.m.; closed Christmas
Fee Area:	No
Restroom:	Yes
Wheelchair/Stroller Access:	No
Drinking Water:	Yes; at visitor center. See Notes/Tips
Picnic Area:	Yes
Lodging:	No
Camping:	No
Suitable for:	All ages. See Notes/Tips

Notes/Tips: Fort/visitor center is 1.5 miles from parking lot, requiring a hike over a rough trail. Best for families with hiking experience. Bring at least one quart of water per person. Wear hiking boots or sturdy, closed-toe shoes, hats and sunglasses. This is rattlesnake habitat, so stay on trail.

Built in just a few weeks, Fort Bowie was an important outpost for U.S. Cavalry troops assigned to fight the Apache led first by Cochise and, eventually, Geronimo. The site today is mostly in ruins. The remains of the fort and the visitor center with it's terrific historical displays are worth investigating.

Fort Bowie National Historical Site, 520-847-2500, Fax: 520-847-2221

13 Cochise Stronghold

Location:	About 10 miles off U.S. Highway 191. See Notes/Tips
Best Time to Visit:	Spring, fall, early winter
Visitor Center/Museum:	No; see Notes/Tips
Hours:	All hours
Fee Area:	$3 for day use; $3 for parking at trail heads; $10 per vehicle/per day for camping
Restroom:	Chemical toilets only
Wheelchair/Stroller Access:	No
Drinking Water:	Yes; see Notes/Tips
Picnic Area:	Yes, at campsites
Lodging:	No
Camping:	Yes
Suitable for:	All ages, but best for experienced campers
Notes/Tips:	Knowledgeable camp hostess on site. Although drinking water is available, I recommend packing in 10-15 gallons

Besides being an honorable man and fierce warrior, legendary Apache Chief Cochise knew how to pick a hideout for his people. Cochise Stronghold, situated in the rugged and unforgiving Dragoon Mountains is, even today, a field trip that is best suited for experienced hikers and campers. But for those up to the challenge, the rewards are spectacular scenery and awesome primitive hiking trails. It is also believed that Cochise was buried near the Stronghold. His grave has never been found.

Cochise Stronghold Campground, 520-364-3468

Slaughter Ranch

14

Location:	On Geronimo Trail, a well-guided dirt road, access from Douglas, and use a good Arizona road map
Best Time to Visit:	Early spring, fall, winter
Visitor Center/Museum:	Yes
Hours:	Wed.-Sun. 10 a.m.-3 p.m.; closed Christmas & New Years
Fee Area:	Yes; adults $3; under 14 free
Restroom:	Yes; barrier free
Wheelchair/Stroller Access:	Yes
Drinking Water:	Yes
Picnic Area:	Yes, shaded tables by a delightful pond
Lodging:	Yes; in nearby Douglas
Camping:	Yes
Suitable for:	All ages

In 1884, famous Texas Ranger, John Slaughter, bought the San Bernardino Ranch, a 100,000 acre spread that reached as far as 20 miles into Mexico. Only a small portion of the historic ranch remains, but the ranch house and other buildings offer a fascinating reminder about what territorial ranching was like for the very wealthy.

Another part of the ranch has been set aside as the San Bernardino National Wildlife Refuge.

This is a must se for any Arizona history enthusiast.

Slaughter Ranch, 6153 Geronimo Trail, Douglas, AZ 85608, 520-558-2474

15
Rex Allen
Arizona Cowboy Museum

Location:	Off AZ 186, about 30 miles northwest of Chiricahua National Monument
Best Time to Visit:	Anytime
Visitor Center/Museum:	Yes
Hours:	Daily 10 a.m.-4 p.m.; closed New Years, Thanksgiving & Christmas
Fee Area:	No; donations suggested & appreciated
Restroom:	Yes
Wheelchair/Stroller Access:	Yes
Drinking Water:	Yes
Picnic Area:	No
Lodging:	Yes; contact: Willcox Chamber of Commerce, 1500 N. Circle I Rd., Willcox, AZ 85643, 520-384-2272
Camping:	No
Suitable for:	All ages

Although he starred in a number of cowboy movies, Rex Allen is best remembered as the narrator for many of the early Walt Disney nature films. "I Love You Arizona", Arizona's official song, was written by Allen.

Located in Willcox's historic district, the Rex Allen Museum and the Willcox Cowboy Hall of Fame pay tribute to the cowboys of the Old West and the rodeo riders of today.

Rex Allen Arizona Cowboy Museum, 155 N. Railroad Ave., Willcox, AZ 85643, 520-384-4583, Fax: 520-384-0851, email: swoutpost@vtc.net

16 Mt. Graham International Observatory

Location:	On State Rte. 366 (Swift Trail) north of Safford
Best Time to Visit:	Summer & early fall
Visitor Center/Museum:	Yes
Hours:	Seasonal; call in advance
Fee Area:	Seasonal & varies with programs; call in advance
Restroom:	Yes; barrier free
Wheelchair/Stroller Access:	Partial; campground is accessible
Drinking Water:	Yes
Picnic Area:	Yes
Lodging:	No
Camping:	Yes
Suitable for:	All ages, best for kids in school
Notes/Tips:	Although kept in good condition, the road to the top of Mt. Graham is somewhat steep, and has many switchbacks. Drive slowly and carefully. Start out with a full tank of gas. Even in the summer, take long pants, closed-toe shoes and warm jackets. Trust me on this. Check local driving conditions during the fall. During the summer, the campground is usually full by Friday morning.

Located high in the Pinaleno Mountains of the Coronado National Forest, Mt. Graham International Observatory features world-class stargazing and astronomical research. Even the Vatican has a telescope at Mt. Graham.

The drive to the top of the mountain takes you through a variety of ecosystems, ranging from cactus and creosote to forests of ponderosa pine, aspens, and fir. A wide variety of wildlife, including the famous Mount Graham red squirrel, deer, and mountain lion live in the high country.

Mt. Graham International Observatory, 1480 W. Swift Trail, Safford, AZ 85546, 928-428-2739

17 Discovery Park's Gov Aker Observatory

Location:	On Discovery Park Blvd. in Safford
Best Time to Visit:	Anytime
Visitor Center/Museum:	Yes
Hours:	Tues.-Sat. 1 p.m.-10 p.m.
Fee Area:	Yes; adults $4; ages 6-11 $3; 5 and under free; train rides $1; flight simulator $6
Restroom:	Yes; barrier free
Wheelchair/Stroller Access:	Yes; except for telescope
Drinking Water:	Yes
Picnic Area:	No
Lodging:	Yes; in Safford
Camping:	No
Suitable for:	All ages; best for kids in school

Serving as the visitor center and gateway to Mt. Graham International Observatory, Gov Aker Observatory is a scientific theme park with something for everyone. The center features displays and hands-on exhibits, but the big attraction is the Polaris Shuttlecraft flight simulator that takes visitors on an imaginary, but realistic journey through space. This fascinating park is a hit with kids and adults alike.

Discovery Park's Gov Aker Observatory, 1651 Discovery Park Blvd., Safford, AZ 85546, 928-428-6260

Northeast Arizona Map

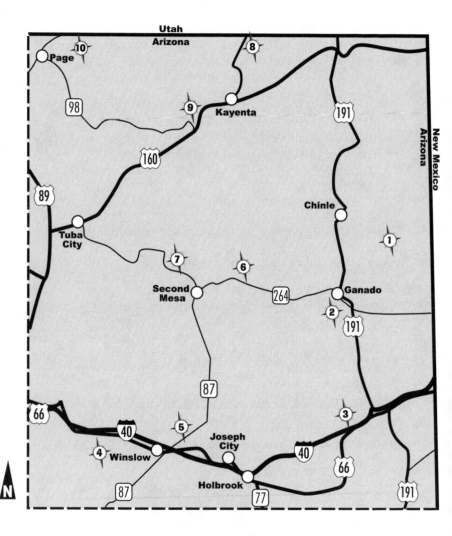

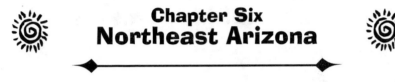

Chapter Six
Northeast Arizona

Sweeping across the northeast part of Arizona, the huge Navajo and smaller Hopi reservations encompass more land than some states.

This multi-colored, other worldly landscape is both forbidding and inspirational. Here, trees have turned to stone, mountains and mesas change color every few minutes, towering arches and rock spires tell of a violent geological past and an enormous wound in the earth warns of a disaster yet to come.

In northeast Arizona, you'll discover vertical cliffs that shelter centuries-old ruins, a lake with more shoreline than the United States west coast, red sandstone cliffs and narrow canyons. You may choose to visit the oldest, continuously inhabited community in the United States where residents perform secret tribal ceremonies unchanged for generations.

Within this sprawling, sparsely populated fantasyland, there are almost twenty national monuments, historic sites and tribal parks, not to mention hundreds of pre-historic ruins. You can explore northeast Arizona from the back of trail horse, on foot, from the deck of houseboat or take a jolting, backcountry ride on a World War II troop transport.

No other region of Arizona is as vast and unforgiving. It's not unusual to drive for several hundred miles through this rugged territory without seeing another living soul. Summers are brutally hot and flash floods are common during monsoon months. When winter storms pound the area, large accumulations of snow aren't unusual. When traveling in northeast Arizona, especially with kids, it's important to be prepared.

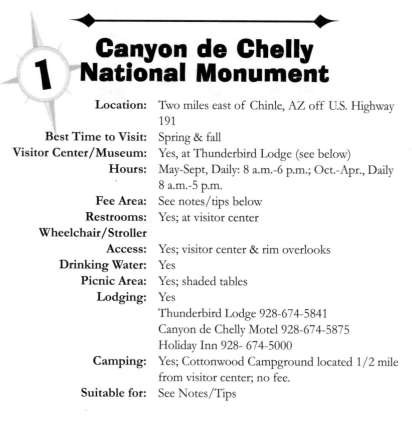

Canyon de Chelly National Monument

Location:	Two miles east of Chinle, AZ off U.S. Highway 191
Best Time to Visit:	Spring & fall
Visitor Center/Museum:	Yes, at Thunderbird Lodge (see below)
Hours:	May-Sept, Daily: 8 a.m.-6 p.m.; Oct.-Apr., Daily 8 a.m.-5 p.m.
Fee Area:	See notes/tips below
Restrooms:	Yes; at visitor center
Wheelchair/Stroller Access:	Yes; visitor center & rim overlooks
Drinking Water:	Yes
Picnic Area:	Yes; shaded tables
Lodging:	Yes
	Thunderbird Lodge 928-674-5841
	Canyon de Chelly Motel 928-674-5875
	Holiday Inn 928- 674-5000
Camping:	Yes; Cottonwood Campground located 1/2 mile from visitor center; no fee.
Suitable for:	See Notes/Tips

Notes/Tips: There is no fee to visit the monument or to drive along rim road and the experience is suitable for all ages. A self-guided hike (two mile round-trip) from the rim to White House Ruins is suitable for kids ages 7 years and older. To explore all other areas of the canyons, you must be accompanied by a Navajo guide. Group tours can be arranged through the Thunderbird Lodge. Guides for private tours (if you own a 4-wheel drive vehicle) can be hired by contacting Thunderbird Lodge. Expect to pay the guide $80 for a full-day tour. It is also customary to provide a sack lunch and soft drinks.

It is illegal to possess or consume alcohol on reservation lands

Canyon de Chelly (pronounced "day shay") National Monument has been described as one of the most serene places in North America. This geological wonderland is really two canyons that connect, forming a "V".

Seen from numerous rim overlooks, the 100 miles of Canyon de Chelly and Canyon del Muerto (Spanish for Canyon of the Dead) appear to be a lost Eden. The sandstone walls are only 30 feet high at the canyon entrance, but rise to over 1,000 feet as both gorges narrow.

For more than 2,000 years, the canyons were home to pre-Columbian Pueblo cultures. The impressive ruins of their cliff dwellings and wonderful examples of rock art are true archaeological treasures. The canyons are also the ancestral home of the Navajo, and many families still farm and herd sheep in the canyon interior.

Canyon de Chelly National Monument, P.O. Box 588, Chinle, AZ 86503, 928-674-5500

Hubbell Trading Post National Historic Site

2

Location:	Off U.S. 191 at Ganado, AZ., 90 minutes northeast of Holbrook
Best Time to Visit:	Late spring, early fall
Visitor Center/Museum:	Yes
Hours:	Daily 8 a.m.-5 p.m.; closed New Years, Thanksgiving & Christmas
Fee Area:	No
Restrooms:	Yes
Wheelchair/Stroller Access:	Yes; excluding parts of Hubbell home
Drinking Water:	Yes
Picnic Area:	Yes; shaded ramadas
Lodging:	No; see Canyon de Chelly National Monument
Camping:	No; see Canyon de Chelly National Monument
Suitable for:	All ages

Even in states with large Native American populations, it's difficult to find an authentic trading post. The Hubbell Trading Post is the genuine article.

Declared a National Historic Site in 1967, the post conducts business with the Navajo in the same way it has for 150 years. Owners of the post buy goods from the Navajo and the Navajo purchase supplies from the post. Tourists buy the Navajo artwork, craftwork and jewelry.

Hubbell is not only a thriving trading center, but a priceless part of Americana. While visiting, be sure to take a tour of the historic John Lorenzo Hubbell home. It includes one of the finest Native American museums in the country.

Hubbell Trading Post National Historic Site, P.O. Box 150, Ganado, AZ 86505, 928-755-3475

Petrified Forest National Park

3

Location:	Off I-40, 25 miles west of Holbrook, AZ
Best Time to Visit:	Fall, Spring, Early Summer
Visitor Center:	Yes; 3
Hours:	Daily 8 a.m.-6 p.m.; closed New Years & Christmas
Fee Area:	Yes; $10 per vehicle
Restrooms:	Yes; barrier-free
Wheelchair/Stroller Access:	Yes; at visitor centers & several hiking trails
Drinking Water:	Yes
Picnic Area:	Yes; at visitor centers.
Lodging:	No; available in Holbrook
Camping:	Wilderness camping only; requires a no-fee National Park permit
Suitable for:	All ages

The Petrified Forest is best known for wood turned to stone and stunning views of the Painted Desert. But just as impressive are the many Triassic-age fossil deposits and ancient Indian ruins.

Most petrified wood deposits are found in the south end of the park from Rainbow Forest up through Blue Mesa. The north end of the park offers the best views of the Painted Desert. A 27-mile paved road winds through this tiny National Park. You'll be directed to many scenic stops and self-guided hiking trails.

There are 3 visitor centers, each offering unique exhibits and interpretative displays. But unlike most National Parks, there are no lodging or camping facilities.

Petrified Forest National Park, Petrified Forest, AZ 86028, 928-524-6228

◆────────────────────────◆

Meteor Crater

Location:	Off I-40 @ exit 233, half-way between Flagstaff and Winslow
Best Time to Visit:	Spring, summer, fall
Visitor Center/Museum:	Yes
Hours:	May 16-Sept. 14, daily 6 a.m.-6 p.m.; Sept. 15-May 15, daily 8 a.m.-5 p.m.
Fee Area:	Yes; $8 adults, $2 ages 6-17, under 6 free
Restrooms:	Yes; barrier-free
Wheelchair/Stroller Access:	Yes; at visitor center only
Drinking Water:	Yes
Picnic Area:	Yes; no shaded ramadas
Lodging:	No; available in Winslow
Camping:	No
Suitable for:	Ages 5 years and older. Younger kids may have to be carried on rim hike.
Notes/Tips:	Wear hiking boots or closed-toed shoes. Sweaters or jackets recommended during cooler months.

50,000 years ago, a small meteorite made a direct hit on northeast Arizona. Impacting the earth with the explosive force of nuclear bomb, everything within a 7-mile radius was leveled, the sun was blotted out and a firestorm blackened the land. What remains of that celestial event is a hole 600-feet deep, almost one mile across and nearly three miles in circumference.

NASA chose Meteor Crater as a training site for the Apollo Moon Landing Program. Visitors to this privately owned park aren't allowed to descend into the crater. A 45-minute guided rim tour is very interesting and serves as a stark reminder of possible future impacts.

Meteor Crater Enterprises, Inc., P.O. Box 0070, Flagstaff, AZ 86002-0070, 928-289-2362

◆━━━━━━━━━━━━━━━━━━━━◆

5 Homolovi Ruins State Park

Location:	Off AZ 87, 8 miles northeast of Winslow
Best Time to Visit:	Spring, summer, early fall
Visitor Center/Museum:	Yes; fine collection of artifacts
Hours:	Daily 8 a.m.-6 p.m.; closed New Years & Christmas
Fee Area:	Yes; $5 per vehicle
Restrooms:	Yes; barrier free
Wheelchair/Stroller Access:	Yes; at visitor center & on hiking trail
Drinking Water:	Yes
Picnic Area:	Yes; shaded ramadas
Lodging:	No; available in Winslow
Camping:	Yes; see Notes/Tips
Suitable for:	All ages
Notes/Tips:	Homolovi State Park Campground is about 1.5 miles off I-40 on AZ 87; 52 sites with electric hookups & dump stations. Water & showers available mid-April thru mid-October. $8 per night for non-hookup, $13 for hookup.

One of the smallest and least visited of Arizona's State Parks, this archaeological site protects ruins dating from A.D. 900, with some of the ancient pueblos containing 700 rooms. The present-day Hopi Indians consider Homolovi sacred and believe their ancestors were the original inhabitants.

A well maintained, self-guided hiking trail winds through the park. Expect to spend about an hour on the trail.

Homolovi Ruins State Park, HC 63, Box 5, Winslow, AZ 86047, 928-289-4106

Keams Canyon Trading Post

6

Location:	Off AZ 264, 50 miles west of Ganado/Hubbell Trading Post
Best Time to Visit:	Spring, summer, early fall
Visitor Center/Museum:	Yes
Hours:	Weekdays 8:30 a.m.-6:30 p.m.; Sat & Sun, 9 a.m.-3 p.m.; closed New Years, Memorial Day, Thanksgiving, Christmas
Fee Area:	No
Restrooms:	Yes; at restaurant
Wheelchair/Stroller Access:	Yes; restaurant only
Drinking Water:	Yes
Picnic Area:	Yes; at trading post & along Keams Canyon rim drive
Lodging:	Yes; see Notes/Tips
Camping:	Primitive only;18 miles west at Second Mesa. Information available at trading post.
Suitable for:	All ages
Notes/Tips:	Would not recommend motel. More comfortable lodging available in Holbrook or Chinle (Canyon de Chelly)

Although not as well known as Hubbell Trading Post, a visit to Keams Canyon is worthwhile just to experience the magnificent natural setting.

Built by Thomas Keam in 1875, the trading post also includes a motel, restaurant, and nearby campground. But exploring tiny Keams Canyon is the big attraction.

Only 8 miles long, a rim road runs along the first three miles of the narrow gorge. Be sure to stop at Inscription Rock where Kit Carson carved his name. There are several charming picnic spots hidden among tall trees.

Keams Canyon Trading Post, P.O. Box 188, Keams Canyon, AZ 86034, 928-738-2296

7 — Oraibi & Hotevilla

Location:	Off AZ 264, about 30 miles west of Keams Canyon Trading Post
Best Time to Visit:	Spring, summer (best time to see cliff gardens @ Hotevilla), early fall
Visitor Center/Museum:	No
Hours:	N/A
Fee Area:	N/A
Restrooms:	Yes; at service stations and restaurants
Wheelchair/Stroller Access:	Yes
Drinking Water:	Yes
Picnic Area:	No
Lodging:	Yes; at Second Mesa; see Notes/Tips
Camping:	Yes; at Second Mesa
Suitable for:	All ages
Notes/Tips:	This is the heart of the Hopi Nation. It is forbidden to visit certain villages, witness certain functions or to photograph certain ceremonies. To avoid conflicts, inquire at the Hopi Cultural Center that includes a clean, well-run restaurant, comfortable motel and campground

Oraibi is the oldest, continuously occupied community in the United States. The first residents settled at the site around A.D. 1150. There are no paved roads and visitors are asked to park outside of town to prevent stirring up dust.

Hotevilla is 4 miles from Oraibi and looks pretty much the same. However, during the summer months the men of the village plant gardens on the side of the surrounding cliffs. The gardens are spectacular and present a wonderful photo opportunity.

Hopi Cultural Center/Motel, Box 67, AZ 264, Second Mesa, AZ 86043, 928-734-2463 or 928-734-2435

Monument Valley Navajo Tribal Park

8

Location:	4 miles off U.S. 163, north of Kayenta, AZ
Best Time to Visit:	May-Sept. (very cold in winter; very hot in summer)
Visitor Center/Museum:	Yes
Hours:	May-Sept daily 7 a.m.-7 p.m.; Oct.-April daily 8 a.m.-5 p.m.; closed New Years, Thanksgiving, Christmas
Fee Area:	Yes; $2.50 per person
Restrooms:	Yes; at visitor center
Wheelchair/Stroller Access:	Yes; at visitor center
Drinking Water:	Yes; see Notes/Tips
Picnic Area:	Yes; some shaded ramadas
Lodging:	No; nearest lodging in Kayenta, AZ (contact the Tribal Park office for information)
Camping:	Yes; developed, group and primitive
Suitable for:	All ages
Notes/Tips:	Take extra drinking water on drive trips. Photography opportunities abound, especially at sunrise & sunset

Thanks to Hollywood, Monument Valley is the most universally recognized landscape in America. The flat-topped buttes and rock spires provided the backdrop for dozens of westerns and television commercials.

The 30,000-acre Monument Valley Navajo Tribal Park boasts a wonderful visitor center/museum that includes a craft shop and exhibits highlighting ancient and recent Native American history.

For a quick explore, take the 18-mile scenic loop drive that begins at the visitor center. But to truly experience the stunning beauty of Monument Valley, consider a Navajo-guided tour. The backroad drive lasts about three hours and costs approximately $15 per person.

Monument Valley Navajo Tribal Park, 801-727-3287

Navajo National Monument

Location:	Off U.S. 160, west of Kayenta, AZ, 10 miles north of Black Mesa Junction on AZ 564
Best Time to Visit:	Spring, Summer, early Fall
Visitor Center/Museum:	Yes
Hours:	Visitor Center: May-early Sept., 8 a.m.-6 p.m.; early Sept.-mid-Dec. & March-May, 8 a.m.-5 p.m.; mid-Dec.-March, 8 a.m.-4:30 p.m.; closed New Years, Thanksgiving, Christmas
Fee Area:	Yes; call for details
Restrooms:	Yes; at visitor center
Wheelchair/Stroller Access:	Yes; at visitor center
Drinking Water:	Yes; at visitor center only
Picnic Area:	Yes; at visitor center & campground
Lodging:	No; nearest lodging in Kayenta, AZ
Camping:	Yes; 30, no fee sites on first-come basis; no hookups or showers
Suitable for:	One-mile Betatakin rim hike for all ages. All other hikes and horseback trips best for experienced hikers ages 10 years and older. Guided hikes/horseback trips to Keet Seel require two months advanced reservations. Contact visitor center for costs.

Established in 1909, Navajo National Monument features wonderfully preserved cliff dwellings built a millennium ago by the Kayenta Anasazi culture. There are two main ruin sites; Betatakin (Navajo for "ledge house") and Keet Seel ("broken pottery").

Sheltered under a high-vaulted alcove, Betatakin ruins overlook a red-rock canyon, forested with oak, fir and aspen. Sandal Trail is a self-guided, one-mile hike that leads to an overlook for a breathtaking view of the ruins. A five-mile ranger-guided hike goes directly to the ruins. The hike takes five-six hours and is rated moderate.

The Keet Seel ruins are, quite simply, overwhelming. Unfortunately, they are only reached only after a **very strenuous** 8.5 mile, overnight hike or horseback trip. For experienced backpackers, Keet Seel is a "must see."

Navajo National Monument, HC 71, Box 3, Tonalea, AZ 86044, 928-672-2366

10 Glen Canyon National Recreation Area/Lake Powell

Location:	Page is 135 north of Flagstaff, off U.S. 89
Best Time to Visit:	Anytime (spring & fall are most popular seasons)
Notes/Tips:	A complete listing of all services, facilities and recreation opportunities available at Page/Lake Powell is beyond the scope of this guide. I recommend consulting a travel agent before planning a trip, or contact: **Lake Powell Marina & Resorts**, P.O. Box 56909, Phoenix, AZ 85079, 602-278-8888 or 800-528-6154

After the completion of Glen Canyon Dam, it took the Colorado River an astounding 17 years to flood the enormous Glen Canyon, creating Lake Powell.

Boasting more shoreline (almost 1,960 miles) than the west coast of the United States and featuring 96 major canyons, countless inlets and coves, exploring and recreation is what Lake Powell is all about. Boating, water-skiing, camping, hiking, fishing, houseboating, championship golf, horseback riding and even scuba diving can all be enjoyed on a family vacation at Lake Powell.

The growing community of Page is the gateway to Lake Powell. Here, you'll find all services, including comfortable lodging, marinas, campgrounds and resorts.

Western Arizona Map

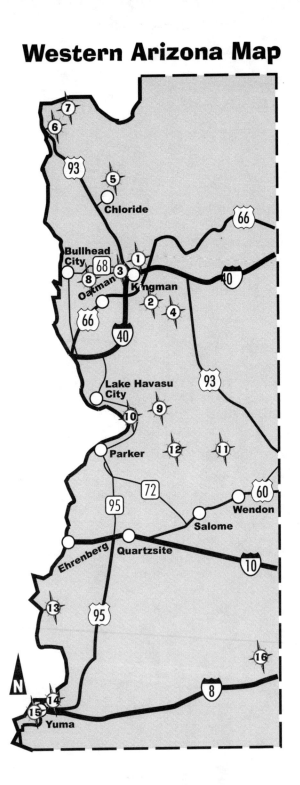

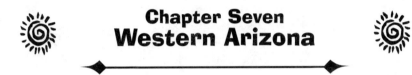

Chapter Seven
Western Arizona

In 1869, Maj. John Wesley Powell, a Civil War hero who lost an arm at the Battle of Shiloh, led the first expedition down the uncharted Colorado River. Using wooden boats, nine men ran the river through a deep scar in the earth that Powell named the Grand Canyon. Only five of the pioneers survived the adventure.

Before Powell's epic journey, maps referred to the Colorado and the western Arizona Territory as "unexplored." In Maj. Powell's own words, Western Arizona was "the great unknown."

Although 50 dams, built in six states, have tried to tame the Colorado, the mighty river still sweeps out of the Grand Canyon creating an aquatic and recreational playground.

Using Kingman and Yuma as the northern and southern gateways to Arizona's river playground, you'll discover Hoover Dam, a mountain of concrete so enormous that most of the cement will never dry. You can spend leisurely days boating, fishing or water skiing on the five beautiful lakes along the Colorado River, including the largest manufactured lake in the country. After a day on the water, why not pitch a tent and spend a night under the stars at one of hundreds of riverfront coves and beaches. If you'd rather be pampered, consider spending a night or two at a world-famous resort and casino. You may choose to visit an old English township, a wildlife sanctuary, ghost towns and a notorious territorial prison.

There are many communities located along the Colorado River where services are available. However, the inland areas of Western Arizona are sparsely populated. Plan carefully for backcountry excursions.

1 Historic Kingman

Notes/Tips: For information regarding lodging & other services, contact: **Kingman Area Chamber of Commerce,** 333 W. Andy Devine Ave., Box 1150, Kingman, AZ 86402, 928-753-6106

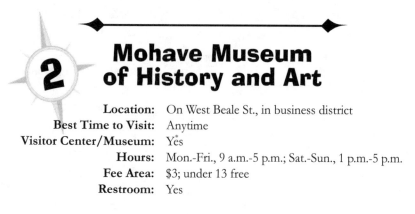

Kingman is the northern hub for visiting Arizona's western regions. Amtrack, Greyhound and America West Airlines all service the community. Interstate 40, U.S. 93, AZ 68 and the longest remaining section of Route 66 all come together in Kingman.

Route 66 is Kingman's main throughfare. The neon-lined roadway has been re-named for native son Andy Devine, the squeaky-voiced actor who played the sidekick in many western movies. Located 186 miles northwest of Phoenix off U.S. 93, Kingman offers comfortable lodging, good restaurants and all services.

The Mohave Museum of History and Arts, Bonelli House and Hualapai Mountain Park are three sites worth investigating.

2 Mohave Museum of History and Art

Location:	On West Beale St., in business district
Best Time to Visit:	Anytime
Visitor Center/Museum:	Yes
Hours:	Mon.-Fri., 9 a.m.-5 p.m.; Sat.-Sun., 1 p.m.-5 p.m.
Fee Area:	$3; under 13 free
Restroom:	Yes

Wheelchair/Stroller
Access: Yes; wheelchair available if needed
Drinking Water: Yes
Picnic Area: No
Suitable for: All ages

Rock hounds will appreciate the excellent mineral display, particularly the Arizona turquoise exhibit. A fascinating diorama tells the strange story of Lt. Edward Beale's comical camel-cavalry unit that went searching for a wagon road to California.

Mohave Museum of History & Arts, 440 W. Beale St., Kingman, AZ 86402, 928-753-3195

3 Bonelli House

Location: On Spring St., in business district
Best Time to Visit: Anytime
Visitor Center Museum: Yes
Hours: Thur.-Mon., 1 p.m.-4 p.m.
Fee Area: No; donations accepted
Restroom: Yes
Wheelchair/Stroller
Access: On first floor only
Drinking Water: Yes
Suitable for: All ages

One of 62 buildings in the business district listed on the National Register of Historic Places, Bonelli House is a fine example of Territorial architecture. Contains many antiques and artifacts.

Bonelli House, 430 E. Spring St., Kingman, AZ 86402, 928-753-3195

4 Hualapai Mountain Park

Location: 15 miles from downtown Kingman on Hualapai Mountain Rd.
Best Time to Visit: Spring, summer, early fall
Visitor Center/Museum: Ranger station only

Hours:	N/A
Fee Area:	For overnight camping only. See Notes/Tips
Restroom:	Yes
Wheelchair/Stroller Access:	Limited access on hiking trails; full access at resort
Drinking Water:	Yes
Lodging:	Yes; contact: Hualapai Mountain Resort, 4525 Hualapai Mountain Rd., Kingman, AZ 86401, 928-757-3545
Camping:	Yes; contact: Hualapai Mountain Park Ranger Station, 928-757-0951
Suitable For:	All ages
Notes/Tips:	Camping is seasonal & fees vary. Haulapai Mt. Resort is open daily except Monday; seasonal rates

Enjoy a 15-mile-drive on Hualapai (pronounced "wall-a-pie") Mountain Road to Hualapai Mountain Park and experience spectacular views from 8,400 feet. Take a day hike or stay overnight at a rustic cabin or campground. If you like being pampered, reserve a room or suite and enjoy fine dining at the Hualapai Mountain Resort.

◆━━━━━━━━━━━━━◆

5 Chloride Ghost Town

Location:	Off U.S. 93, 15 miles north of Kingman
Best Time to Visit:	Spring, fall, winter
Visitor Center/Museum:	Yes
Hours:	N/A
Fee Area:	No
Restroom:	Yes; at Chloride Town Park on Second St.
Wheelchair/Stroller Access:	Yes
Picnic Area:	Yes; at Chloride Town Park
Lodging:	B&B & RV park only
Camping:	Yes; in the Cerbat Mts. @ Windy Pt. & Pack Saddle campgrounds
Suitable For:	All ages

Named for the silver ore that was mined in the area, Chloride was a rowdy territorial mining camp. When the silver played out, Chloride fell on hard times. Only a few hardy souls now call this dusty community home. What remains of this almost ghost town are its historic treasures.

You'll find a huge bank vault that is now a small museum, the old Tennessee Saloon and the well preserved Jim Fritz house, built in 1890.

Don't miss the giant murals that western artist, Roy Purcell, painted on boulders on the outskirts of town.

Chloride Chamber of Commerce, P.O. Box 268, Chloride, AZ 86431, 928-656-2204, e-mail: chloride.arizona@juno.com

6 Hoover Dam

Location:	Off U.S. 93, 65 miles northwest of Kingman, AZ
Best Time to Visit:	Spring & Fall
Visitor Center/Museum:	Yes; two facilities
Hours:	Memorial Day-Labor Day, daily 8 a.m.-7:30 p.m. (last guided tour @ 6:15 p.m.); rest of the year, daily 9 a.m.-5 p.m. (last guided tour @ 4:15 p.m.)
Fee Area:	Yes; entrance fee & guided tour $6 per person
Restroom:	Yes
Wheelchair/Stroller Access:	Yes; including guided tours
Drinking Water:	Yes
Picnic Area:	No
Lodging:	No; nearest lodging @ Boulder City, Nevada
Camping:	No
Suitable for:	All ages
Notes/Tips:	U.S. 93 from Kingman to Hoover Dam is a narrow road with hairpin curves; drive carefully

One of the true architectural wonders of the world, Hoover Dam is visually and statistically mind-numbing. You simply can't ignore Hoover Dam; it's just too damn big!

Statistically, Hoover Dam:

1) is the largest concrete dam in the Western Hemisphere; 727 feet high & 660 feet thick

2) contains 4.5 million yards of concrete - enough to build a two-lane road from coast-to-coast

3) has so much concrete poured, that much of the interior will **never dry**

Your visit to Hoover Dam should include the guided tour that takes you deep inside the structure for a close-up look at its internal workings. Tours depart every few minutes from the visitor center located on the top of the dam. The larger Alan Bible Visitor Center on the Nevada side of the dam houses an interpretative gallery, impressive observation tower and a movie theater with three revolving sections.

Hoover Dam @ Lake Mead, Bureau of Reclamation, P.O. Box 60400, Boulder City, NV 89006-0400, 702-293-8367

Alan Bible Visitor Center, 601 Neveda Hwy., Boulder City, NV 89005, 702-293-8906

7 Lake Mead National Recreation Area

Location:	At Hoover Dam; see above
Best Time to Visit:	Spring & Fall
Visitor Center/Museum:	Yes
Suitable For:	All ages
Notes/Tips:	Space prohibits listing all of the services, lodging and camping options. For information, contact: **Alan Bible Visitor Center,** 601 Neveda Hwy., Boulder City, NV 89005, 702-293-8906

Formed in 1935 with the completion of Hoover Dam, Lake Mead is the largest manufactured body of water in the United States. Lake Powell boasts more shoreline, but at 105 miles in length with a surface area of 229 square miles, Lake Mead takes top honors.

Wide and placid, Lake Mead attracts sailors, jet-skiers, water-skiers, speed-boaters, houseboaters, anglers (professional & amateur), campers and scuba divers.

The National Park Service oversees all activities at Lake Mead National Recreation Area. There are full service marinas with no-fee boat launching at Overton Beach, Boulder Beach, Callville Bay and Echo Bay. Lake Mead Cruises offer a 90-minute water tour of the lake and Hoover Dam area aboard a 250-passenger stern-wheeler. Gray Line Tours offers a 15-mile motorized raft trip down the Colorado River from the base of Hoover Dam.

Oatman Ghost Town

8

Location:	Off old Route 66 (now U.S. 68), 35 miles southwest of Kingman. The last 15 miles offer a "white-knuckle" dirt-road ride through the Black Mountains.
Best Time to Visit:	Spring, fall, winter
Visitor Center/Museum:	Yes
Hours:	N/A
Fee Area:	No
Restroom:	Yes; in motel & shops
Wheelchair/Stroller Access:	Yes; in most parts of the town
Drinking Water:	Yes
Picnic Area:	No
Lodging:	Yes; at the Old Oatman Hotel. Bathroom & shower "down the hall." Family-style restaurant open until 3 p.m. Contact: Old Oatman Hotel, P.O. Box 38, Oatman, AZ 86433, 928-768-4408
Camping:	No
Suitable for:	All ages

A few folks still reside in the former gold mining town of Oatman. You'll find three open saloons and the Oatman Hotel where Clark Gable and Carole Lombard honeymooned after their secret wedding in Kingman. The big attraction is the wild burros that often wander down Main Street. If you want to feed them, you can buy hay from the general store.

9 Lake Havasu State Park

Location:	50 miles southwest of Kingman on AZ 95
Best Time to Visit:	Early spring, fall & winter; summers are very hot
Visitor Center/Museum:	Yes
Hours:	6 a.m. - 10 p.m. daily except Christmas
Fee Area:	Yes; $6 per vehicle
Restroom:	Yes; at Visitor Center
Wheelchair/Stroller Access:	Yes; at Visitor Center
Drinking Water:	Yes; at Visitor Center and campground
Picnic Area:	Yes; shaded ramadas
Lodging:	Yes; in Lake Havasu City. Contact: Lake Havasu City Visitor & Convention Bureau, 1930 Mesquite Ave., Suite 3, Lake Havasu City, AZ 86402, 928-453-3444 or 800-242-8278
Camping:	Yes; $12 per site; no electric hook-ups
Suitable for:	All ages

When the famous London Bridge began to sink, the City of London put the structure, all 10,000 tons of it, up for sale. Entrepreneur Robert McCulloch bought the bridge, hoping that it would be become the crowd-drawing centerpiece of a community he planned to build on the shores of Lake Havasu. McCulloch's gamble paid off. Today, Lake Havasu City and nearby Lake Havasu State Park are popular recreational sites that offer houseboating, water skiing, jet-boating, camping, fishing and hiking to old mines and the Havasu National Wildlife Refuge.

Lake Havasu State Park, 1801 Hwy. 95, Lake Havasu City, AZ 86406, 928-855-2784

Cattail Cove State Park

10

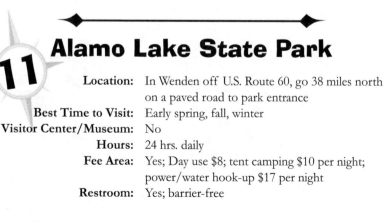

Location:	15 miles south of Lake Havasu City off AZ 95
Best Time to Visit:	Early spring, fall, winter
Visitor Center/Museum:	Yes; including a marina & restaurant
Hours:	24 hrs. daily
Fee Area:	Day use $8; tent camping $12 per night; electric hook-up $17 per night
Restroom:	Yes; barrier-free
Wheelchair/Stroller Access:	Yes
Drinking Water:	Yes
Picnic Area:	Yes; some ramadas
Lodging:	No
Camping:	Yes; including water/electric hook-up, tables, grills, showers and RV/trailer dump station
Suitable for:	All ages

Cattail Cove State Park offers the convenience of full-service camping along with the solitude of a campsite accessible only by boat.

Along the shores of Lake Havasu, you'll find secluded coves, great fishing, lakeside camping, a large boat ramp and boat rentals. If you appreciate a quiet, relaxing outdoor experience without sacrificing creature comforts, Cattail Cove is a sure winner.

Cattail Cove State Park, P.O. Box 1990, Lake Havasu City, AZ 86405, 928-855-1223

Alamo Lake State Park

11

Location:	In Wenden off U.S. Route 60, go 38 miles north on a paved road to park entrance
Best Time to Visit:	Early spring, fall, winter
Visitor Center/Museum:	No
Hours:	24 hrs. daily
Fee Area:	Yes; Day use $8; tent camping $10 per night; power/water hook-up $17 per night
Restroom:	Yes; barrier-free

Wheelchair/Stroller
Access: Yes
Drinking Water: Yes
Picnic Area: Yes; with ramadas
Lodging: No
Camping: Yes
Suitable for: All Ages

Noted for excellent bass and catfish angling, Alamo Lake State Park also features full-service camping, picnicking, water sports and wildlife watching.

You can rent a boat and fishing tackle at the supply store or launch your own craft at the boat ramp. The first-rate campgrounds include water and electric hook-up, grills, showers, tables and dump stations. You'll find miles of hiking trails winding through scenic desert hills. Kids will appreciate the large playground.

Alamo Lake State Park, P.O. Box 38, Wenden, AZ 85357, 928-669-2088

Buckskin Mountain State Park & River Island Unit

Location: Off AZ 95, 11 miles north of Parker
Best Time to Visit: Early spring, fall, winter
Visitor Center/Museum: No
Hours: 24 hrs. daily
Fee Area: Day Use $8; camping $17 per night; cabanas (covered campsites) $22 per night; fees waived on Christmas Day
Restroom: Yes; barrier-free
Wheelchair/Stroller
Access: Yes
Drinking Water: Yes
Picnic Area: Yes; with ramadas
Lodging: No
Camping: Yes; including power, water, showers and dump station
Suitable for: All ages

Located on the banks of the mighty Colorado River, Buckskin Mountain State Park offers a variety of water sports, camping and three sensational hiking trails.

Two units, the River Island Unit and Buckskin Point, provide waterfront ramadas and sandy beaches. Wonderful hiking trails lead to the top of bluffs that provide memorable views of the Colorado River. A concession-operated market carries a wide variety of products as well as water sports equipment rental.

Buckskin Mountain State Park & River Island Unit, 5476 Hwy. 95, Parker, AZ 85344, 928-667-3231

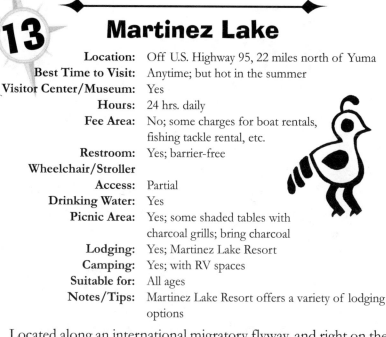

13 Martinez Lake

Location:	Off U.S. Highway 95, 22 miles north of Yuma
Best Time to Visit:	Anytime; but hot in the summer
Visitor Center/Museum:	Yes
Hours:	24 hrs. daily
Fee Area:	No; some charges for boat rentals, fishing tackle rental, etc.
Restroom:	Yes; barrier-free
Wheelchair/Stroller Access:	Partial
Drinking Water:	Yes
Picnic Area:	Yes; some shaded tables with charcoal grills; bring charcoal
Lodging:	Yes; Martinez Lake Resort
Camping:	Yes; with RV spaces
Suitable for:	All ages
Notes/Tips:	Martinez Lake Resort offers a variety of lodging options

Located along an international migratory flyway, and right on the Colorado River, Martinez Lake offers some of the best bird watching in the state. The restored estuary is a lush riparian habitat supporting numerous species of sport fish (huge catfish often landed), giving anglers hours of great fun. Water sports enthusiasts can enjoy jet skiing, kayaking, water skiing, canoeing, and driving pontoon boats on the lake or Colorado River.

Martinez Lake, 928-783-9589 or 800-876-7004 (both numbers connect with resort)

◆━━━━━━━━━━━━━━━━━━━━━━━━━◆

Yuma Territorial Prison State Historical Park

14

Location:	Off I-8 at exit 1, just west of downtown Yuma
Best Time to Visit:	Early spring, fall & winter
Visitor Center/Museum:	Yes
Hours:	8 a.m.-5 p.m. daily; closed Christmas
Fee Area:	Yes; 14 & older, $4; 7-13, $3; 6 & under, free
Restroom:	Yes
Wheelchair/Stroller Access:	Yes; entire complex
Drinking Water:	Yes
Picnic Area:	Yes; shaded ramadas
Lodging:	Not on park grounds. Numerous hotels & motels in Yuma. Contact: Yuma Convention & Visitors Bureau, 377 S. Main St., Box 10831, Yuma, AZ 85366, 928-783-0071
Camping:	No
Suitable for:	All ages

Between 1867 and 1909, more than 3,000 men and women served time at the Yuma Territorial Prison. Built mostly by convicts, the notorious jail featured tiny cells that held up to six inmates each. By today's standards, the prison was a hell hole. But during territorial times, when prisoners at other facilities were often subjected to beatings and food rationing, the Yuma inmates weren't roughed-up and food was plentiful. The prison even included a hospital and library. In 1961, the complex was declared a State Historic Park.

Yuma Territorial State Historic Park, 1 Prison Hill Rd., Yuma, AZ 85364 928-783-4771

15 Yuma Crossing State Historic Park

Location:	On North Fourth Ave. in Yuma
Best Time to Visit:	Early spring, fall & winter
Visitor Center/Museum:	Yes
Hours:	10 a.m.-5 p.m. daily; closed Christmas
Fee Area:	Yes; adults $4; ages 7-13 $3; 6 and under free
Restroom:	Yes; barrier free
Wheelchair/Stroller Access:	Yes
Drinking Water:	Yes
Picnic Area:	Yes; with some shaded tab;es
Lodging:	Not on grounds; available in Yuma.
Camping:	No
Suitable for:	All ages; most appreciated by kids in school

From prehistoric times until the Colorado River was bridged, this site was the only crossing point over the lower Colorado. Over time, native peoples, Spanish missionaries, gold seekers, mountain men, settlers, and the U.S. Army depended on the crossing.

In the 1860s the army built a Quartermaster Depot here to provide supplies to army outposts. Today, visitors to this fascinating park can explore the remains of the historic buildings. The park also features a transportation museum, stagecoaches, and mule wagons. This is one stop every Arizona history enthusiast should put on their agenda.

Yuma Crossing State Historic Park, 201 N. Fourth Ave., Yuma, AZ 85364 928-329-0471

16 Painted Rocks Park

Location:	Go 30 miles west of Gila Bend on I-8. Exit on Painted Rocks Rd. & go 15 miles to park
Best Time to Visit:	Fall, winter
Visitor Center/Museum:	No; camp host on site during winter months
Hours:	24 hrs.
Fee Area:	No fee to visit park; $4 per night for camping.
Restroom:	Yes
Wheelchair/Stroller Access:	Yes; but can be difficult
Drinking Water:	No
Picnic Area:	Yes
Lodging:	No
Camping:	Yes
Suitable for:	All ages
Notes/Tips:	Remote area; nearest services, food and water in Gila Bend. Best for experienced campers. Be alert for rattlesnakes

A solitary hill in an otherwise flat landscape, Painted Rocks Park contains the heaviest concentration of petroglyphs in the Southwest. Chiseled on the rocks almost a 1,000 years ago by the Hohokam people, many of the images were painted, hence the name.

The Bureau of Land Management oversees the park and a self-guided discovery trail has been recently completed. You can examine an incredible display of rock pictures, including animal figures, humans, reptiles and abstractions that still puzzle archaeologists.

There is a small, primitive campground and a nearby reservoir that should NOT be used for swimming or as a source of drinking water. This is a remote site but worth the time to investigate.

No on-site contact information or address. Suggest contacting: Bureau of Land Management, 2015 W. Deer Valley Rd., Phoenix, AZ 85027, 623-580-5500

Western Arizona

East–Central Arizona
and White Mountains Map

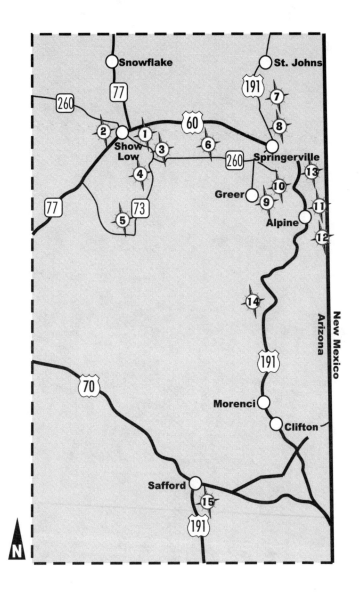

Chapter Eight
East–Central Arizona and White Mountains

Diversity might best describe east-central Arizona and the beautiful White Mountains. Captivating views, fragrant pine forests and a variety of summer and winter recreational opportunities beckon Arizona travelers. Fishing, camping, hiking, wildlife watching and photography are a few of the most popular summer activities. Winter offers sledding, downhill and cross-country skiing, snowshoeing, snowmobiling and ice fishing.

On our discovery of east-central Arizona, we'll re-trace the route of Spanish explorer Coronado literally traveling from "palms to pines" in a few breathtaking hours. After conquering an 11,000 foot mountain, we'll learn why the Vatican was so interested in building an observatory on Mt. Graham. In a land that has been occupied for more than 10,000 years, we'll investigate an ancient ruin that overlooks the Little Colorado River and we might un-earth a 700 year-old "talking pot."

Some of the best fishing lakes and streams are found in the White Mountains. With a little luck, we'll catch fat rainbow trout and maybe a brilliantly colored Apache trout. If not, we'll find them by the millions in their holding tanks at two remarkable hatcheries.

Our adventure begins in a forest community where an ownership feud resulted in the town being named after a game of chance. Down the road apiece, we'll make snow angels or enroll in a "guaranteed to ski in one day" class at the state's largest ski area. At the eastern end of the White Mountains, midway between the state's northern and southern borders, lies Alpine. Here, you might want to take in the sheep dog trials, or wager a few bucks on worm race day.

Show Low

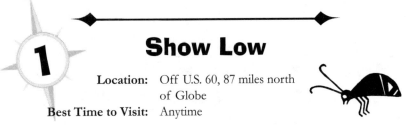

Location: Off U.S. 60, 87 miles north of Globe

Best Time to Visit: Anytime

When it comes to settling disputes, Arizonans are a creative bunch. Ranchers Corydon Cooley and Marion Clark felt that there wasn't enough room in the state for both of them. To decide who would move, they played a card game called Seven Up. Low card takes the hand. "If you show low, you win," Clark reputedly said to Cooley. Drawing a deuce of clubs, Cooley said, "show low it is." The site of the card game became the town of Show Low.

Show Low is a gateway to east-central Arizona and the White Mountains. In this quiet mountain community, you'll find comfortable lodging, good restaurants and other services. Using the town as a base, you can discover a number of nearby attractions and enjoy a host of outdoor activities. The Show Low Chamber of Commerce will forward information about their charming town.

Show Low Chamber of Commerce, P.O. Box 1083, Show Low, AZ 85901-1083, 928-537-2326, www.showlow.com

Fool Hollow Lake Recreation Area

2

Location:	About 6 miles northwest of Show Low off Fool Hollow Lake Rd.
Best Time to Visit:	Summer & fall
Visitor Center/Museum:	No
Hours:	Campground gates: 5 a.m.-10 p.m.; host office: 8 a.m.-5 p.m.; closed Christmas Day
Fee Area:	Single day $5 per vehicle; tent camping $10 per vehicle per day; electric hook-up $15 per vehicle per day
Restroom:	Yes; barrier-free
Wheelchair/Stroller Access:	Yes
Drinking Water:	Yes
Picnic Area:	Yes
Lodging:	In nearby Show Low
Camping:	Yes
Suitable for:	All ages

At this tiny mountain lake you can enjoy trout fishing, boating, canoeing and excellent camping. The recreation area includes tent camping sites, electrical hook-ups for trailers and RVs, two handicapped boat docks and four playgrounds. Lucky anglers might catch their limit of plump rainbow trout.

Fool Hollow Lake Recreation Area, 1500 Fool Hollow Lake Rd., Show Low, AZ 85901, 928-537-3680

Pinetop-Lakeside

3

Location:	Off AZ 260, 15 miles southeast of Show Low
Best Time to Visit:	Summer, early fall
Visitor Center/Museum:	Yes
Hours:	Chamber: Mon.-Fri. 9 a.m.-5 p.m.; Sat.-Sun. 10 a.m.-2 p.m.
Fee Area:	No

Restroom:	Yes
Wheelchair/Stroller Access:	Entire community
Drinking Water:	Yes
Picnic Area:	Yes
Lodging:	Yes; a variety of options
Camping:	No
Suitable for:	All ages

On a weekend visit to the twin towns of Pinetop and Lakeside, you'll have the opportunity to purchase outstanding Arizona produce from a number of fruit and vegetable stands that line the main streets. Popular retirement and vacation communities, Pinetop and Lakeside also features two delightful bed & breakfast inns, resorts, lodges and cottages and a trailhead that connects with the magnificent General Crook Historic Trail. Good trout fishing is available at nearby Rainbow Lake.

Pinetop/Lakeside Chamber of Commerce, P.O. Box 4220, Pinetop, AZ 85935, 928-367-4290

◆————————————◆

Williams Creek and Alchesay National Fish Hatcheries

4

Location:	Wiiliams Creek Hatchery: Off Williams Creek Hatchery Rd., 12 miles southeast of Pinetop-Lakeside; Alchesay Hatchery: Off AZ 73, about 15 miles south of Pinetop-Lakeside
Best Time to Visit:	Summer, early fall
Visitor Center/Museum:	small information offices
Hours:	Weekdays 7:30 a.m.-3 p.m.; weekends & holidays with prior arrangements
Fee Area:	No
Restroom:	Yes; but locked after hours
Wheelchair/Stroller Access:	Yes; restrooms are small but manageable
Drinking Water:	Yes
Picnic Area:	At Alchesay Hatchery only

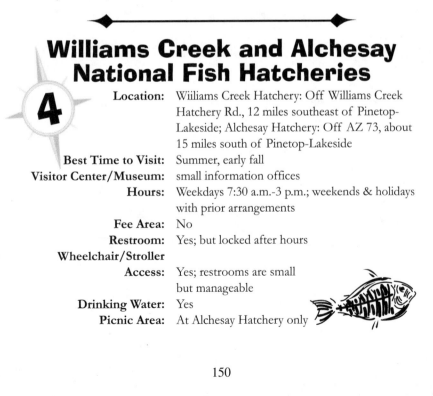

Lodging: No
Camping: No
Suitable for: All Ages

Arizona's only native trout was once on the brink of extinction. Today, the golden-yellow Apache trout that rarely exceeds 10 inches, is making a dramatic recovery. Apache trout are now raised at the Williams Creek and Alchesay National Fish Hatcheries. Once restricted to small, headwater streams in the White Mountains, the Apache are being introduced to other streams outside of their natural range.

At both facilities you'll find self-guided walkways and visitor information. Williams Creek also features a terrific wildlife viewing deck that overlooks a pond. Besides seeing millions of trout, you might also spot a bald eagle, osprey, wild turkey or a bull elk.

Williams Creek National Fish Hatchery, 928-334-2346
Alchesay National Fish Hatchery, 928-338-4901

5 Kinishba Ruins

Location:	Drive 15 miles west of Whiteriver on AZ 73. Look for a sign, turn right and go 4 miles to the ruins
Best Time to Visit:	Summer, early fall
Visitor Center/Museum:	No
Hours:	Anytime
Fee Area:	No
Restroom:	No
Wheelchair/Stroller Access:	No
Drinking Water:	No
Picnic Area:	No
Lodging:	No
Camping:	No
Suitable for:	All ages
Notes/Tips:	Removing or damaging ruins or artifacts is a federal crime and a downright rotten thing to do. Keep an eye open for rattlesnakes and don't step or reach where you can't see.

Kinishba was a large masonry pueblo built and occupied by the Anasazi culture between about A.D. 1050 and 1350. The complex may have had a population of 2,000 and had strong and effective leadership.

Most of the Kinishba site is fenced off and few people take the time to visit this special ruin. The site is administered by the Fort Apache Tribe and permission is not needed to visit the ruins. You'll be on your own and there are no interpretive centers or facilities. But for amateur archaeologists and pre-Columbian history enthusiasts, this ruin is worth investigating.

Kinishba Ruins, White Mountain Apache Tribe Office of Tourism, Box 710, Ft. Apache, AZ 85926, 928-338-1230

◆━━━━━━━━━━━━━━━━━━━━◆

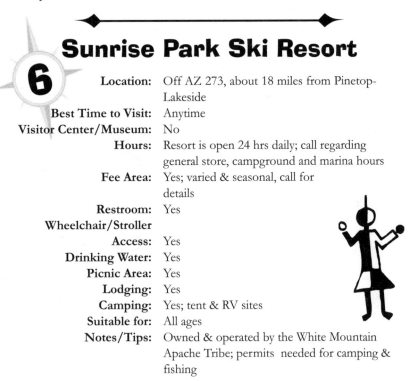

Sunrise Park Ski Resort

6

Location:	Off AZ 273, about 18 miles from Pinetop-Lakeside
Best Time to Visit:	Anytime
Visitor Center/Museum:	No
Hours:	Resort is open 24 hrs daily; call regarding general store, campground and marina hours
Fee Area:	Yes; varied & seasonal, call for details
Restroom:	Yes
Wheelchair/Stroller Access:	Yes
Drinking Water:	Yes
Picnic Area:	Yes
Lodging:	Yes
Camping:	Yes; tent & RV sites
Suitable for:	All ages
Notes/Tips:	Owned & operated by the White Mountain Apache Tribe; permits needed for camping & fishing

Besides being Arizona's largest ski resort, Sunrise Park Resort is a year-round outdoor recreation playground. Winter skiing is excellent with 11 lifts and 65 trails on three mountains. Summer activities include fishing and boating at Sunrise Lake, hiking, camping, mountain biking, horseback riding and scenic lift rides.

The Sunrise Park Resort Lodge features 100 rooms, Tempest Dining Room, lounge, pool, Jacuzzi and sauna. A general store sells groceries, clothing, camping and fishing supplies and Apache Reservation camping and fishing permits. Boat rentals, fishing equipment & bait available at Sunrise Lake Marina.

Sunrise Park Resort, P.O. Box 217, McNary, AZ 85930, 800-772-7669 or 928-735-7669, www.sunriseskipark.com

Lyman Lake State Park

Location:	Off U.S. 180, 11 miles south of St. Johns & 13 miles north of Springerville
Best Time to Visit:	Summer & early fall
Visitor Center/Museum:	Yes
Hours:	Visitor Center: 8 a.m.-5 p.m. daily; campground 24 hrs. daily; open all holidays
Fee Area:	Yes; day use $5 per vehicle; tent camping $12 per vehicle per night; electric hook-up $17 per vehicle per night
Restroom:	Yes; barrier-free
Wheelchair/Stroller Access:	Yes
Drinking Water:	Yes
Picnic Area:	Yes
Lodging:	No; available in St. Johns & Springerville
Camping:	Yes; tent and RV sites
Suitable for:	All ages

A small dam on the Little Colorado River created Lyman Lake, a high plains hideaway that is home to a herd of buffalo. Lyman Lake State Park offers great fishing, camping, hiking and unrestricted water sports.

Water skiers can challenge a unique slalom course. Ranger-guided hikes along the impressive petroglyph (1,000 year-old rock art) trail are very popular. Anglers might catch trout, bass, catfish or pike.

Lyman Lake State Park, P.O. Box 1428, St. Johns, AZ 85936, 928-337-4441

8 Casa Malpais

Location:	In Springerville on East Main St.
Best Time to Visit:	Anytime
Visitor Center/Museum:	Yes; with outstanding exhibits
Hours:	Sun.-Mon. 7:30 a.m.-5 p.m.; Tues.-Sat. 7:30 a.m.-7 p.m.
Fee Area:	Yes; Adults $4; 55 & up $3; 12-18 $3; under 12 $1
Restroom:	Portable toilets only
Wheelchair/Stroller Access:	No; hiking trails are narrow, rocky and ascend 250-300 vertical feet; toilets aren't accessible. Visitor center/museum will accommodate chairs
Drinking Water:	Yes
Picnic Area:	No
Lodging:	See Notes/Tips
Camping:	No
Suitable for:	Kids in early grade school should appreciate the ruins and the hike. Younger kids may be challenged by the hike and bored with the narrative provided by the guide.
Notes/Tips:	Wear hiking boots or sturdy, closed-toe shoes. Bring hats, sunglasses & water bottles. If hike becomes too difficult, don't hesitate to inform the guide.

Springerville is a friendly town located about 15 east of the New Mexico border, where U.S. 60 & AZ 260 meet. You'll find good restaurants, comfortable lodging and all other services. So that you have time to see many of the sites in the region, I recommend spending a night or two in Springerville. The Round Valley Chamber of Commerce will gladly send a visitor packet to you.

Inhabited by the Mogollon people between about A.D. 1250 and 1400, the ruins of Casa Malpais ("badlands house") is unlike most other ruins in the Southwest. This masonry pueblo has more than fifty rooms, a ceremonial kiva, residential apartments and a huge stone wall that surrounds the entire group of ruins. There are pre-historic trails, stairways that lead to the top of a cliff, walls of petroglyphs and very rare underground ceremonial chambers.

Almost 600 years after being abandoned, the pueblo remains virually intact. A one mile round-trip interpretive hiking trail winds through the park. Guides must accompany visitors and hikes are scheduled daily at 9 and 11 a.m. and 2 p.m. You should visit the wonderful museum before beginning your tour. Casa Malpais should be included on discovery of east-central Arizona.

Casa Malpais, 318 East Main Street, Springerville, AZ 85938, 928-333-5375
Round Valley Chamber of Commerce, Box 31, Springerville, AZ 85938, 928-333-2123

9 Greer/Greer Lakes

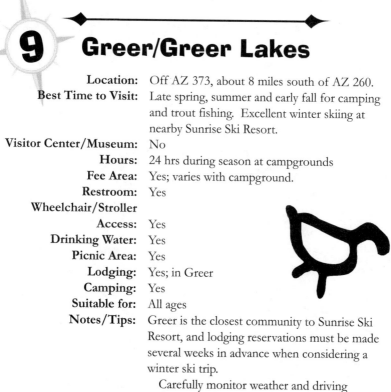

Location:	Off AZ 373, about 8 miles south of AZ 260.
Best Time to Visit:	Late spring, summer and early fall for camping and trout fishing. Excellent winter skiing at nearby Sunrise Ski Resort.
Visitor Center/Museum:	No
Hours:	24 hrs during season at campgrounds
Fee Area:	Yes; varies with campground.
Restroom:	Yes
Wheelchair/Stroller Access:	Yes
Drinking Water:	Yes
Picnic Area:	Yes
Lodging:	Yes; in Greer
Camping:	Yes
Suitable for:	All ages
Notes/Tips:	Greer is the closest community to Sunrise Ski Resort, and lodging reservations must be made several weeks in advance when considering a winter ski trip.
	Carefully monitor weather and driving conditions before planning a trip to Greer, especially during the winter months.

Located at 8,500 feet, the alpine community of Greer is often called the Jewel of the White Mountains. In this beautiful forested area, you'll find excellent lake and stream fishing, outstanding hiking, equestrian and mountain biking trails, cross-country and exciting downhill skiing and wildlife viewing opportunities.

Greer offers the city-dweller peace and quiet, relaxation and clear pine-scented air. This charming community also boasts great dining and picturesque alpine lodging facilities.

Within a mile of downtown Greer, you'll find Bunch, River and Tunnel Reservoirs collectively known as the Great Lakes. During the summer months, anglers can fish for rainbow and brown trout from the shore or from a boat. Ice fishing is popular during the winter. There are three campgrounds near the lakes that are open from about May 1st through Labor Day, weather permitting.

Round Valley Chamber of Commerce, Box 31, Springerville, AZ 85938, (928) 333-2123.

White Mountain Apache Office of Tourism: (928) 338-1230

Road & Weather Information: (928) 537-ROAD (7623)

10 Coronado Trail Scenic Byway

The Coronado Trail Scenic Byway (U.S. 191) covers a distance of 123 miles from Springerville in the north to Morenci in the south. This is reputed to be the trail taken by Francisco Vasques de Coronado over four centuries earlier in his quest for the Seven Cities of Cibola. The route passes through some of the most magnificent countryside in east-central Arizona.

Keep in mind that the road is steep and narrow in places, with plenty of sharp curves. If visiting during the winter, please contact local authorities for current weather and driving conditions or restrictions.

Along the way, let's make stops at Alpine, Luna Lake and Hannigan Meadows.

11   Alpine

Location:	Off U.S. 191, 24 miles south of Springerville
Best Time to Visit:	Anytime; see Notes/Tips
Visitor Center/Museum:	Yes; at chamber office
Lodging:	Yes; call for details
Camping:	Yes; call for details
Suitable for:	All ages
Notes/Tips:	If planning a winter visit, prepare for winter driving conditions. Be well supplied and check weather and driving conditions before departure.

At an elevation of 8,050 feet, the captivating highland community of Alpine is often called the "Alps of Arizona." Here, there are four distinct seasons to delight tourists with varied scenery and activities.

Winter sports include organized events such as dog sled races, ice fishing derbies and "Winterfest" competitions in snow sculpture, sledding and cross-country skiing. Summer diversions consist of golfing one of the highest 18-hole courses in the country, mountain biking, trout fishing and camping.

You'll find comfortable lodges, inns, RV parks, campgrounds and restaurants. Request an information from the Chamber of Commerce

Alpine Area Chamber of Commerce, P.O. Box 410, Alpine, AZ 85920, 928-339-4330

Road & Weather Information 928-537-ROAD (7623)

Luna Lake

Location:	Of U.S. 180, 4 miles east of Alpine
Best Time to Visit:	Summer, early fall
Visitor Center/Museum:	No
Hours:	Seasonal; call ahead
Fee Area:	Yes; $8.65 non-refundable camping reservation fee, $8 per night
Restroom:	Yes; barrier-free
Wheelchair/Stroller Access:	Yes; most areas around the lake, including marina
Drinking Water:	Yes
Picnic Area:	Yes
Lodging:	Not at lake
Camping:	Yes; tent & small trailer, but no electric hook-ups
Suitable for:	All ages
Notes/Tips:	I suggest making camping reservations through the National Camping Reservation Network. Excellent resource for camping questions or reservations anywhere in the United States

Camping, boating, hiking, mountain biking and excellent trout fishing are all activities to be enjoy at picturesque, 80-acre Luna Lake. Facilities include a small marina with boat and fishing tackle rentals, convenience store and pleasant campground.. Anglers often catch a limit of trout and big fish are common. Many animals frequent the area, including herds of elk.

Luna Lake Yacht Club, Alpine, AZ 85920, No phone, FAX only 928-339-4323

National Camping Reservations, 877-444-6777

Escudilla Mountain/Wilderness

13

Location:	Off U.S. 191, about 21 miles south of Springerville
Best Time to Visit:	Summer, fall
Visitor Center/Museum:	No
Hours:	N/A
Fee Area:	No
Restroom:	No
Wheelchair/Stroller Access:	No
Drinking Water:	No
Lodging:	No
Camping:	Yes; see Notes/Tips
Suitable for:	All ages; see Notes/Tips
Notes/Tips:	This is a wilderness experience best suited for experienced hikers. Remember to follow all wilderness rules: pack it in, pack it out; stay on designated trails; leash pets; no motorized or mechanical vehicles; pack animals allowed; observe all posted precautions regarding re-introducing Mexican gray wolves. Take plenty of water and trail snacks. Prepare for high country hiking.

Escudilla Mountain, or as it translates from Spanish, soup bowl, looks more like a soup bowl turned upsided-down. At almost 11,000 feet, it is the third highest peak in Arizona. Here you can hike through groves of aspen, spruce, fir, ponderosa pine, Gambel oak, and Rocky Mountain maple. Many types of animals inhabit this wilderness, including wolves, black bear, elk, and deer. The 3.3 Escudilla National Recreation Trail is the most popular hike in the wilderness. Beginning at Terry Flat, the trail ascends to a fire lookout tower near the mountain's summit.

Escudilla Mountain/Wilderness, 928-339-4384

Hannagan Meadow

14

Location:	Off U.S. 191, 23 miles south of Alpine
Best Time to Visit:	Anytime; check weather & driving conditions before a winter visit
Visitor Center/Museum:	No
Hours:	24 hrs. daily
Fee Area:	Yes; call for rates
Restroom:	Yes, barrier-free
Wheelchair/Stroller Access:	Yes
Drinking Water:	Yes
Lodging:	Yes
Camping:	Yes; call for details
Suitable for:	All ages
Notes/Tips:	For moms & dads looking for a romantic get-away without the kids, Hannagan Meadow Lodge rates serious consideration

If there is a heaven on earth, Hannagan Meadow may be the headquarters. Located in a lush meadow, surrounded by towering pines, you'll discover sensational Hannagan Meadow Lodge. This log lodge is about all you'll find at Hannagan Meadow, but if you're hankering for a little peace and quiet in one of the most beautiful spots in Arizona, I encourage you to spend a night. The food is wonderful and the cabins all have wood-burning stoves that add to the already special ambiance. Some cabins are also equipped with kitchens. In the early morning, it' not unusual to see elk and deer feeding on the tall grass only a few yards from your cabin.

Hannagan Meadow Lodge, HC 61, Box 335, Alpine, AZ 85920, 928-339-4370 or 800-547-1416, www.hannaganmeadow.com

✦━━━━━━━━━━━━━━━━━━━✦

Roper Lake State Park

15

Location:	Off U.S. 191, 4 miles south of Safford
Best Time to Visit:	Spring, summer, early fall
Visitor Center/Museum:	Small information center
Hours:	Information center: 8 a.m.-5 p.m. daily except Christmas; campground: 24 hrs. daily
Fee Area:	Day use $5 per vehicle; tent camping $12 per vehicle per night; electric hook-up $17 per vehicle per night
Restroom:	Yes; barrier-free
Wheelchair/Stroller Access:	Yes
Drinking Water:	Yes
Picnic Area:	Yes
Lodging:	Not at park; lodging & services available in Safford
Camping:	Yes
Suitable for:	All ages

Visitors to this small state park located near towering Mount Graham can swim, fish, camp and enjoy a dip in a rock-lined hot tub. Roper Lake State Park features full-service camping with restrooms, showers, dump station, water and electric hook-up, fire rings, grills and tables. There are numerous picnic ramadas for day use, many hiking trails and a boat ramp.

Roper Lake State Park, 101 E. Roper Lake Rd., Safford, AZ 85546, 928-428-6760

North-Central Arizona Map

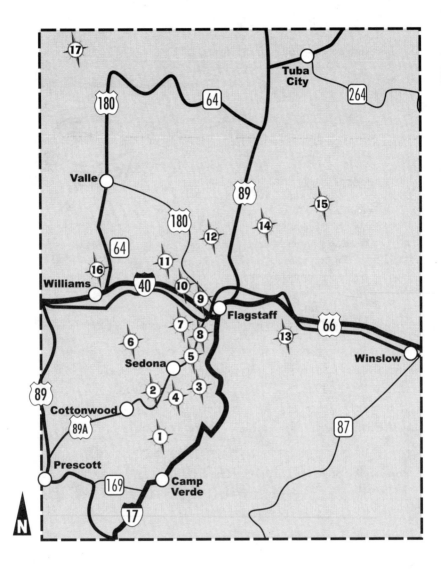

Chapter Nine
North-Central Arizona

A land of dynamic contrast, north-central Arizona is recognized worldwide for its stunning natural beauty, exciting destinations and numerous outdoor recreation opportunities.

Journeying through this land of stunning red rock formations and old growth forests, you'll discover a mountain that blew its top with the explosive force of an atomic bomb. At Slide Rock State Park, you can slide on your backside down a narrow chute in a mountain stream. If camping, hiking, fishing and backpacking are on your agenda, visiting four unique state parks will do the trick.

Arizona's north-central region has been inhabited for 10,000 years. Here, you'll find mysterious ruins with strange names like Wukoki, Lomaki, Nalakihu and Wupatki that bear silent testimony to the construction talents of "Those Without Water" and the "Alien Ancient Ones." At Walnut Canyon National Monument a switchback hiking trail along the edge of deep canyon will take us to dwellings hidden in caves and limestone alcoves.

Sedona and Flagstaff are the popular starting points for a tour of the region. Annually, over 4 million visitors stop at Sedona to marvel at the surrounding rock formations and nearby canyons. On our visit to Sedona, we'll take a doorless jeep to a seldom-visited canyon on the Verde River.

Prior to the completion of Interstate 40, millions of people passed through Flagstaff when driving coast-to-coast along historic Route 66. Today, Flagstaff is a thriving community and home to the Northern Arizona University Lumberjacks. Featuring comfortable lodging and fine dining, Flagstaff also boasts a number of attractions worth investigating. On our discovery, we'll scan the universe with a century-old telescope and visit a mansion once owned by Flagstaff's first logging barrons. We won't miss the Pioneer Historical Museum or the sensational Museum of Northern Arizona. After a few relaxing days spent in Flagstaff, let's ride the rails to the Grand Canyon and prepare to fight off an outlaw gang.

Before setting up operations in Sedona and Flagstaff, let's make a quick stop in Cottonwood in the beautiful Verde Valley.

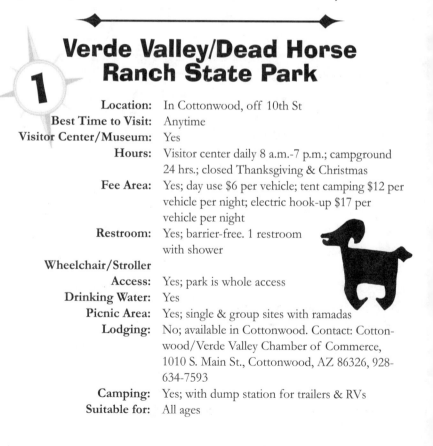

Verde Valley/Dead Horse Ranch State Park

1

Location:	In Cottonwood, off 10th St
Best Time to Visit:	Anytime
Visitor Center/Museum:	Yes
Hours:	Visitor center daily 8 a.m.-7 p.m.; campground 24 hrs.; closed Thanksgiving & Christmas
Fee Area:	Yes; day use $6 per vehicle; tent camping $12 per vehicle per night; electric hook-up $17 per vehicle per night
Restroom:	Yes; barrier-free. 1 restroom with shower
Wheelchair/Stroller Access:	Yes; park is whole access
Drinking Water:	Yes
Picnic Area:	Yes; single & group sites with ramadas
Lodging:	No; available in Cottonwood. Contact: Cottonwood/Verde Valley Chamber of Commerce, 1010 S. Main St., Cottonwood, AZ 86326, 928-634-7593
Camping:	Yes; with dump station for trailers & RVs
Suitable for:	All ages

Camping, fishing, hiking and outstanding bird watching are just a few of the recreational pursuits available at Dead Horse Ranch State Park. Located in the scenic Verde Valley, this lush riparian (water-based) habitat supports more than 100 bird species and 350 native plant species.

There are 45 first-come first-served campsites with tables, grills, electricity, water, restrooms and a shower. Hiking trails begin near the shaded picnic area and wind along the banks of the Verde River. This is an excellent place to spot wildlife. In the four-acre lagoon, anglers will find catfish, panfish and bass. Trout are often stocked in the winter.

Dead Horse Ranch State Park, 675 Dead Horse Ranch Rd., P.O. Box 144, Cottonwood, AZ 86326, 928-634-5283

Page Springs Hatchery

2

Location:	4 miles off AZ 89A, about 12 miles south of Sedona
Best Time to Visit:	Spring, summer; fall is best when leaves change color
Visitor Center/Museum:	Yes
Hours:	Daily 7:00 a.m.-4:00 p.m.; closed Thanksgiving & Christmas
Fee Area:	No; Arizona's hatcheries are supported primarily by fishing license sales
Restroom:	Yes
Wheelchair/Stroller Access:	Yes
Drinking Water:	Yes
Picnic Area:	Yes
Lodging:	No
Camping:	No
Suitable for:	All ages

One place where you can always see up to a million pan size trout is north-central Arizona's Page Springs Hatchery. Several springs located near the facility produce a constant flow of 15 million gallons of water a day that enters the hatchery where 300,000 pounds of rainbow trout are raised annually.

Besides trout, this riparian area is home to amphibians, reptiles, mammals and is one of the best bird watching spots in north-central Arizona. The hatchery features a wonderful visitor center and a viewing/feeding pond that is especially popular with kids.

Page Springs Hatchery, 1600 N. Page Springs Rd., Cornville, AZ 86325, 928-634-4805

3 ◆ Red Rock State Park

Location:	On Lower Red Rock Loop Rd., 5 miles west of Sedona off AZ 89A
Best Time to Visit:	Anytime
Visitor Center/Museum:	Yes
Hours:	Winter: 8 a.m.-6 p.m.; summer: 8 a.m.-7 p.m.; closed Thanksgiving & Christmas
Fee Area:	$6 per vehicle
Restroom:	Yes
Wheelchair/Stroller Access:	Visitor center, but very limited on grounds
Drinking Water:	Yes
Picnic Area:	Yes
Lodging:	No
Camping:	No
Suitable for:	All ages
Notes/Tips:	Specialized programs, theater, classroom and limited overnight facilities are available for groups on a reservation basis

A nature center dedicated to providing environmental education programs for kids and adults, Red Rock State Park features outstanding exhibits, interpretive programs and superb ranger-led hikes.

Surrounded by the red rocks near Sedona, this diverse riparian habitat created by Oak Creek, supports a variety of plants and wildlife. There is no overnight camping (see Notes/Tips), pets aren't allowed and visitors must remain on designated roads and trails.

There are day use picnic sites with charcoal grills, but open fires and wood gathering are prohibited.

Red Rock State Park, HC 02, Box 886, Sedona, AZ 86336, 928-282-6907, FAX: 928-282-5972

◆ V-Bar-V Ranch Rock Art Site

4

Location:	On FR 618, 2.8 miles east of I-17 & Exit 298 (the Sedona exit)
Best Time to Visit:	Anytime
Visitor Center/Museum:	Yes
Hours:	Fri.-Mon. 9:30 a.m.-4:30 p.m.; gates close at 3:30 p.m.
Fee Area:	Yes; adults $3; Golden Age & Golden Access $1.50; under 16 free
Restroom:	Yes; well-maintained, sanitary portables
Wheelchair/Stroller Access:	With a little effort, the short, wide trail to the rock art panels could be accessible, provided the ground isn't wet. It's a judgment call.
Drinking Water:	No; bring water bottles
Picnic Area:	No; but a day picnic area is located opposite Beaver Creek Campground, located about 1/4 mile from the site.
Lodging:	No
Camping:	Yes; at nearby Beaver Creek Campground which is open year-round
Suitable for:	All ages; most appreciated by kids in school
Notes/Tips:	Please keep in mind that touching ancient petroglyphs damages the rock art. Your guide will be watching.

On thirteen vertical rock walls/panels, the prehistoric Sinagua left a remarkable record of their travels that is the largest known, and best-preserved example of rock art in the Verde Valley.

Your discovery begins at the small visitor center that houses artifacts and information about the amazing Sinagua people. Departing the center, you'll take a .4-mile walk to the rock art location.

Along the way, you'll find ruins of the original ranch house, including the brick chimney where you still can see the ranch's V-Bar-B brand.

At the petroglyph panels, a guide will host fascinating discussions about the mysterious rock art.

V-Bar-B Ranch Rock Art Site, Friends of the Forest, 928-204-2594

5 Sedona

Superlatives can't begin to describe the wondrous red rock cliffs and canyons of world-renowned Sedona.

Annually, more than 4 million visitors come to marvel at the dreamscape of red rock spires, deep gorges and mountain streams or to browse and shop in the boutiques and art shops. Weekends and holidays can be extremely crowded. For a more rewarding discovery, I suggest a mid-week visit.

There are so many things to see in Sedona proper, they can't all be listed. After arriving, stop at the Sedona-Oak Creek Canyon Chamber of Commerce and pick up a walking-tour map. Plan your visit to allow enough time for other attractions outside of town that are highlighted below.

Sedona-Oak Creek Canyon Chamber of Commerce, 331 Forest Rd. (at the corner of N. Hwy. 89A), Box 478, Sedona, AZ 86339, 928-282-7722 or 800-288-7336, Mon.-Sat. 9 a.m.-5 p.m.; Sun. 9 a.m.-3 p.m.

6 Tlaquepaque

Location:	On Highway 179 (after the "Y" intersection) in Sedona
Best Time to Visit:	Anytime
Visitor Center/Museum:	Yes; sort of
Hours:	Varies depending on the establishment
Fee Area:	No
Restroom:	Some great ones
Wheelchair/Stroller Access:	Yes

Drinking Water:	Yes
Picnic Area:	No, not exactly. However, you'll find dining patios at restaurants
Lodging:	Plenty in Sedona
Camping:	No; available in nearby Oak Creek
Suitable For:	All ages

If you enjoy shopping and fine dining, indulge yourself at beautiful Tlaquepaque. Here, you can stroll and shop for unique items in one of the many fascinating shops with a Southwest theme and merchandise. It's very Santa Fe-like.

The restaurants offer a variety of choices from fancy dining to casual. Prices all over the board, so I suggest that you check the menu before deciding.

Tlaqupaque hosts the annual Sedona Holiday Light Festival, a juried event where families set up Christmas displays that are truly unique and elaborate. This is a holiday event that is definitely worth experiencing.

Tlaquepaque, Highway 179, Sedona

7 Sedona Red Rock Jeep Tours

Location:	Departs from tour office in "Uptown Sedona" on N. Hwy. 89A
Best Time to Visit:	Spring, late summer, fall, early winter
Visitor Center/Museum:	No
Hours:	Standard tours daily; Cave Dwellings of the Ancients by reservation
Fee Area:	Yes; varies with tour. Inquire when making reservations
Restroom:	Portable toilets at one location on archaeological tour
Wheelchair/Stroller Access:	Some standard tours with advanced notice; not on archaeological excursions
Drinking Water:	Yes; but bring water bottles

Picnic Area:	Yes; on most tours
Lodging:	In Sedona
Camping:	Yes
Suitable For:	Standard tours: all ages; archaeological tours: 10 yrs. & older recommended

I'm not big on organized tours, jeep or otherwise. But with some advanced notice, you can arrange a private adventure to sensational ancient cliff dwellings along the East Verde River.

Red Rock Jeep Tours offer a host of guided tours of the Sedona region, most lasting an hour or two. But the "Cave Dwellings of the Ancients" archaeological excursion is dynamite. Weather and river conditions permitting, it even includes some easy canoeing on the scenic Verde River. After a backroad drive through miles of magnificent red rock country, you'll walk or canoe to an ancient Sinaguan ("Those Without Water") culture archaeological site. The limestone cliffs above the river House nearly 100 cave dwellings with some 400 rooms in all. Arrowheads and pottery shards can be found. The guides are knowledgeable and friendly. Make reservations and ask about necessary items to bring along.

Sedona Red Rock Jeep Tours, P.O. Box 10305, Sedona, AZ 86339, 928-282-6826 or 800-848-7728, FAX: 928-282-0254

Palatki and Honanki Ruins

Location:	30 miles west of Sedona off Boynton Pass Rd.; a dirt road that is suitable for passenger cars unless the road is wet. Honaki is about 4. 5 miles beyond Palatki. Contact the Sedona Ranger Station (see next page) to obtain a map.
Best Time to Visit:	Anytime
Visit Center/Museum:	Yes
Hours:	Daily except Christmas; 9:30 a.m.-4:30 p.m.; gates close at 4 p.m.
Fee Area:	Free if you have purchased a Red Rock Pass. Otherwise: $5 per car; discounts for Golden Age

& Golden Access members; ages 16 & under
free; Golden Eagle Pass *not* honored

Restroom: Yes; barrier free

Wheelchair/Stroller
Access: Limited primarily to visitor center(s) and short
portions of hiking trails

Drinking Water: Yes; however, I suggest bringing water bottles

Picnic Area: No

Lodging: No

Camping: No

Suitable for: Ages about 6 and older; some easy hiking
involved

Palatki, meaning "Red House" and Honanki, meaning "Bear House," were first reported and excavated by Dr. Jesse Walter Fewkes in 1895. The Southern Sinagua Indians inhabited both of these remarkable sites. They lived here from 1100 AD to about 1300 AD. These prehistoric pueblos are two of the largest and best-preserved cliff dwellings in the Verde Valley. Both ruin sites also included wonderful petroglyphs and pictographs dating back to about 8,000 years. At Palatki, you'll see unique black rock paintings. At Honanki, look for a petroglyph of Kokopelli, the hump-backed flute player who is thought to have been a trickster, womanizer, and fertility figure.

Palatki & Honanki Ruins, Sedona Ranger District, 928-282-4119 or Palatki-Red Cliffs, 928-282-3854

9 Slide Rock State Park

Location: Off AZ 89A, 7 miles north of Sedona

Best Time to Visit: Summer

Hours: winter 8 a.m.-5 p.m.; spring 8 a.m.-6 p.m.;
summer 8 a.m.-7 p.m.

Fee Area: Yes; $6 per vehicle up to 4 people; $2 for each
additional person

Restroom: Yes

Wheelchair/Stroller
Access: Very limited; would not advise

Drinking Water:	Yes
Picnic Area:	Yes
Lodging:	No
Camping:	No
Suitable for:	Kids should know how to swim; diligent parental supervision is a must
Notes/Tips:	Before enjoying the water slide, change into crummy jeans and old sneakers. Park is exceptionally crowded on summer weekends and holidays. Suggest making this a mid-week adventure.

Located on the grounds of an historic apple farm nestled in Oak Creek Canyon, Slide Rock State Park contains one of the Canyon's most famous and exciting attractions. A 30-foot water slide worn in the rocks cuts through the creek bed creating a natural chute.

This beautiful park offers not only thrilling natural water sliding, but bird watching, historic interpretive exhibits and some of the best-tasting apples south of Washington State.

10 Along Oak Creek Canyon Road

Location:	Between Sedona & Flagstaff
Best Time to Visit:	Summer & fall
Notes/Tips:	Lots of traffic, particularly in summer; drive carefully. Contact Sedona-Oak Creek Chamber of Commerce above for camping & lodging information.

The late Charles Krault, host of the long-running CBS "On The Road" series, once observed that with the completion of the Interstate Highway System, it's possible to drive almost anywhere in the country and not see a thing.

I-17 is the most direct route from the southern deserts to Flagstaff. It's also boring. Oak Creek Canyon Road (AZ 89A), on the other hand, is a sensational backcountry drive between Sedona and Flagstaff.

Covering a distance of about 25 miles, the road twists and turns through the stunning canyon, providing marvelous views of the region's red rock cliffs. When the leaves change color in the fall, the drive is breathtaking.

Along the way, you'll spot a number of delightful campgrounds, lodges and inns.

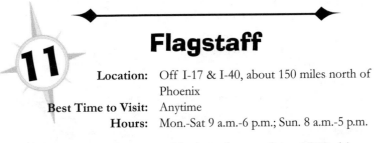

Flagstaff

Location:	Off I-17 & I-40, about 150 miles north of Phoenix
Best Time to Visit:	Anytime
Hours:	Mon.-Sat 9 a.m.-6 p.m.; Sun. 8 a.m.-5 p.m.

Made instantly famous with the release of the 1950s hit recording *Get Your Kicks on Route 66*, Flagstaff is located at the base of the towering San Francisco Peaks, Arizona's tallest mountain range.

Called the Gateway to the Grand Canyon, many tourists simply pass through Flagstaff or stay a single night on their way to Arizona's most famous natural wonder. But Flagstaff is a vibrant community featuring a variety of impressive attractions that are worth discovering.

With a population of nearly 45,000, Flagstaff boasts fine restaurants, lodging ranging from modest motels to posh resorts, world-class skiing and four seasons.

For a complete run-down on services and amenities, contact or visit the Flagstaff Visitor Center.

Flagstaff Visitor Center, 1 E. Rt. 66, Flagstaff, AZ 64001, 928-774-9541 or 800-842-7293

Riordan State Historic Park

Location:	On Riordan Ranch St., near Northern Arizona University in Flagstaff
Best Time to Visit:	Anytime
Visitor Center/Museum:	Yes
Hours:	May-Sept. daily 8 a.m.-5 p.m.; Oct.-Apr. daily 11 a.m.-5 p.m. See Notes/Tips
Fee Area:	Yes; $4 per person; 12 and under free
Restroom:	Yes
Wheelchair/Stroller Access:	Limited to first-floor rooms and surrounding grounds
Drinking Water:	Yes
Lodging:	Not at park
Camping:	No
Suitable for:	All ages; best for kids 8 yrs. & older
Notes/Tips:	Guided tours only, normally beginning on the hour; call ahead

Logging help build Flagstaff and a wonderful reminder of the town's early years can be discovered at Riordan State Historic Park.

Logging kings Timothy and Michael Riordan married two sisters. In 1904, the couples moved into a huge mansion that was the talk of the Arizona Territory. A portion of the whooping 40-room, 13,300-square-foot showcase home was occupied by family members until 1986.

This unique "arts and crafts" mansion and pristine historical log-and-stone structure filled with original furnishings, is an impressive reminder of high-society-living in a small logging town.

Riordan State Historic Park, 1300 Riordan Ranch St., Flagstaff, AZ 86001, 928-779-4395

13 Lowell Observatory

Location:	On Mars Hill Rd., 2 miles from downtown Flagstaff
Best Time to Visit:	Summer
Visitor Center/Museum:	Yes
Hours:	Seasonal; call first
Fee Area:	Yes; 18 & up $3.50; 5-17 $1.50; under 5 free
Restroom:	Yes
Wheelchair/Stroller Access:	Yes
Drinking Water:	Yes
Picnic Area:	No
Lodging:	No
Camping:	No
Suitable for:	All ages; telescope viewing best for ages 8 yrs. & older
Notes/Tips:	The dome is open and the facility isn't heated. Dress warmly.

On a clear night in 1930, astronomer Clyde Tombaugh scanned the outer limits of the solar system with his telescope at Lowell Observatory. He saw a small flicker of light which he realized was the ninth planet called Pluto, thought to exist but never observed.

Today, Lowell Observatory is open to stargazers of all ages and is an experience that I highly recommend.

The fabulous Steele Visitor Center features daytime slide presentations, tours and several interactive exhibits for kids, including the enjoyable Pluto Walk, a solar system tour. Weather permitting (except during January and February), evening visitors can peer through a 24-inch, 100 year-old telescope. Viewing through the Tombaugh Pluto telescope is also included.

Lowell Observatory, 1400 W. Mars Hill Rd., Flagstaff, AZ 86001, 928-774-2096

Pioneer Historical Museum

14

Location:	On Fort Valley Rd., northwest of downtown Flagstaff
Best Time to Visit:	Anytime
Visitor Center/Museum:	Yes; museum gift shop is worth investigating
Hours:	Mon.-Sat. 9 a.m.-5 p.m.; closed major holidays
Fee Area:	No; donations are appreciated
Restroom:	Yes
Wheelchair/Stroller Access:	Limited to 1st floor
Drinking Water:	Yes
Picnic Area:	Yes
Lodging:	No
Camping:	No
Suitable for:	All ages; best for ages 8 yrs. & older

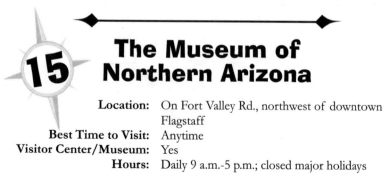

Fine exhibits and displays highlighting the history of Flagstaff are housed in the Pioneer Historical Museum, a rock building constructed in 1908.

The facility was Coconino County's first hospital for the indigent. One display includes an iron lung and a turn-of-the-century doctor's office. You'll also discover exhibits that focus on the region's logging industry, as well as crafts, quilts and hundreds of dolls and teddy bears. The folk-craft festival held over the July Fourth holiday is educational and entertaining.

Pioneer Historical Museum, 2340 N. Fort Valley Rd., Flagstaff, AZ 86001, 928-774-6272

The Museum of Northern Arizona

15

Location:	On Fort Valley Rd., northwest of downtown Flagstaff
Best Time to Visit:	Anytime
Visitor Center/Museum:	Yes
Hours:	Daily 9 a.m.-5 p.m.; closed major holidays

Fee Area:	Yes; $5 per person
Restroom:	Yes; barrier-free
Wheelchair/Stroller Access:	Yes
Drinking Water:	Yes
Picnic Area:	Yes
Lodging:	No
Camping:	No
Suitable for:	All ages

Located only a few blocks from the Pioneer Museum, the Museum of Northern Arizona is a "must see."

Displays on the geology, biology, archaeology, ethnohistory and fine arts of the area are outstanding. Although only about 1 percent of the museum's holdings are on display at a given time, allow the better part of day to take in the sights, exhibits and interactive programs. Permanent exhibits include a stunning collection of Navajo rugs and a Hopi kiva. A new exhibit, devoted primarily to kids, includes a life-size model of Dilophosaurus, a meat-eating dinosaur. Guided tours of the museum are available with a two week advanced notice. Nature trail hikes are offered during the summer.

The Museum of Northern Arizona, 3001 N. Fort Valley Rd., Flagstaff, AZ 86001, 928-774-5213

16 Arizona Snowbowl

Location:	8 miles off U.S. 180 on Snowbowl Rd.
Best Time to Visit:	Anytime
Visitor Center/Museum:	No
Hours:	Seasonal; call ahead
Fee Area:	Yes; seasonal & varied
Restroom:	Yes
Wheelchair/Stroller Access:	Depends upon your requirements and choice of activities; call ahead
Drinking Water:	Yes
Picnic Area:	Yes
Lodging:	Yes
Camping:	Yes

Suitable for:	All ages
Notes/Tips:	Contact Arizona Snowbowl for detailed information regarding lodging, services, programs & prices

Popular year-round, Arizona Snowbowl offers excellent winter skiing and breathtaking views in the summer.

Ski season normally begins in November with some runs open as late as mid-April. A number of ski packages are available, including the "learn to ski in a day" program and the SKIwee program for kids ages 4-8. In the summer, a few of the ski trails are open to mountain bikers. One ski lift is converted to a skyride that climbs to a height of 11,500 feet, offering spectacular views of the North Rim of the Grand Canyon. Nearby Hart Prairie Lodge offers equipment rental and instruction.

Arizona Snowbowl, P.O. Box 40, Flagstaff, AZ 86002-0040, 928-779-1951 or 800-828-7285, www.arizonasnowbowl.com

17 Lava River Cave

Location:	Off FS 171A, 13.5 miles from Flagstaff, via Highway 180; not difficult to find (locals can point the way), but and area roadmap helps
Best Time to Visit:	Spring, summer, fall
Visitor Center/Museum:	No
Hours:	Daylight hours; plan to be out of the cave before sundown
Fee Area:	No
Restroom:	No
Wheelchair/Stroller Access:	No
Drinking Water:	No
Picnic Area:	No
Lodging:	No
Camping:	No
Suitable for:	Ages 6 & older
Notes/Tips:	This a **dark** cave, and may frighten very young kids. Take at least *two* quality flashlights (with

new batteries) per person. Long pants, hiking
boots or sturdy, closed-toe shoes a must. As the
cave is chilly, a light jacket is suggested. I also
strongly encourage wearing bicycle helmets. Take
it from me, I drilled my skull on the cave roof.

The area surrounding Flagstaff is called the San Francisco Volcanic Area. This cave is evidence of the violent volcanic activity that formed Arizona's tallest mountain (Mt. Humphreys), and litter the landscape with volcanic rocks.

Entering the subterranean lava tunnel is the most difficult part of teh 3/4 mile-long hike. To access the main cave, you will need to climb over some pretty big boulders.

It doesn't take long for the natural light to vanish, and your only source of light will be your flashlight. In the glow of your torch you discover strange rock formations, and marvel as you imagine the natural forces that created this tunnel. You'll be able to walk upright for most of the hike. However, at one point you'll have to duck walk for about 20 feet as the caves ceiling is only about three feet high (remember the tip about helmets).

The cave will fork not long before reaching the end of the tunnel. You can go either way, as the forks come back together at the end of the tunnel. Return the same way.

Lava River Cave, on FS 171A

◆━━━━━━━━━━━━━━━◆

18 Walnut Canyon National Monument

Location:	7.5 miles east of Flagstaff off I-40, take a 3-mile road south to the monument. A sign on I-40 is easy to spot
Best Time to Visit:	Spring, summer, fall
Visitor Center/Museum:	Yes
Hours:	Daily 8 a.m.-5 p.m.; closed Thanksgiving & Christmas
Fee Area:	Yes; $4 per vehicle
Restroom:	Yes; barrier-free

Wheelchair/Stroller Access:	Visitor center & rim hikes are accessible; Island Trail is not
Drinking Water:	Yes
Picnic Area:	Yes; only at designated picnic grounds
Lodging:	No
Camping:	No
Suitable for:	All ages; best for kids ages 8 & older (see Notes/Tips)
Notes/Tips:	Portions of the Island Trail are on the edge of the canyon cliff. Parents, position yourself between your child and the drop-off and **hold your child's hand**. Wear hiking boots or closed-toe shoes. Have a water bottle for each person. The monument is at 7,000 ft. and the Island Trail includes a 185-foot vertical ascent. If you're a little out of shape, or have an existing heart condition, go slowly and use caution. Take advantage of the bench stops along the trail. If in doubt, enjoy the easy, scenic rim trail and excellent views from the visitor center.

One of the prettiest spots in north-central Arizona, Walnut Canyon National Monument features striking examples of ancient cliff dwellings and cave homes.

The pine-shaded canyon is small and not particularly deep. The pre-Columbian Sinagua culture built their homes in the numerous caves and alcoves found on the canyon walls. The Sinagua began constructing their canyon fortress around A.D. 1125, but mysteriously abandoned the site around 1400.

Your first stop should be the visitor center which houses outstanding exhibits and artifacts. Massive picture windows look out over the gorge. Through fixed binoculars you can examine a number of the rock and adobe dwellings.

If you're up to it (see Notes/Tips), take the sensational 3/4- mile round trip Island Trail hike along the canyon cliffs. The trail leads to 25 of the cliff dwelling rooms; from the trail, you can see about 100 others.

Walnut Canyon National Monument, Walnut Canyon Rd., Flagstaff, AZ 86004, 928-526-3367

Two Guns Ghost Town

19

Location:	Right off I-40 (Can be seen on the south side of freeway) 30 miles east of Flagstaff
Best Time to Visit:	Spring, summer, fall
Visitor Center/Museum:	No
Hours:	Daylight hours
Fee Area:	No
Restroom:	No
Wheelchair/Stroller Access:	No
Drinking Water:	No
Picnic Area:	No
Lodging:	No
Camping:	No
Suitable for:	Ages 7-8 and older
Notes/Tips:	First of all, you'll be technically trespassing when you visit this historic site. This ghost town is on private land, however, if you are respectful, don't damage property or fences, a discovery is okay. You will know you are at the right place when you spot the abandoned KOA campground, and the huge cowboy waving two six•z guns.

This is rattlesnake country; watch your step, and don't put your hands where you can't see. There are many deep fissures and old mine pits; watch the kids closely. **Do not** try to walk acorss any of the old bridges.

Two Guns, and nearby Canyon Diablo were raucous and lawless railroad towns where the daily violence made the murder and mayhem in Tombstone seem like child's play. But long before the white man moved in, there were hostilities taking place right at the present site of Two Guns between the Apache and their cousins, the Navajo. In fact, there was an incident in the labyrinth of caves that Two Guns is built upon that resulted in the fiery death of a score of Apache braves. To this day, the Navajo consider Two Guns to be haunted.

The remains of the old buildings and abandoned mines of Two Guns can be explored safely, provided you don't get too close to the shafts or natural fissures. You can also safely enter a few of the buildings, but look for snakes that might be lounging in the shade.

Read up on the fascinating history of Two Guns and Canyon Diablo before you visit..

Two Guns Ghost Town, Off I-40, 30 miles east of Flagstaff

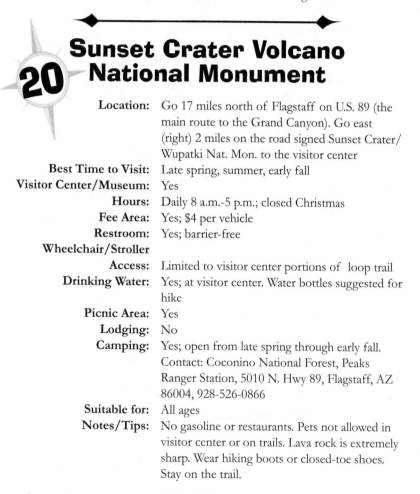

Sunset Crater Volcano National Monument

Location:	Go 17 miles north of Flagstaff on U.S. 89 (the main route to the Grand Canyon). Go east (right) 2 miles on the road signed Sunset Crater/Wupatki Nat. Mon. to the visitor center
Best Time to Visit:	Late spring, summer, early fall
Visitor Center/Museum:	Yes
Hours:	Daily 8 a.m.-5 p.m.; closed Christmas
Fee Area:	Yes; $4 per vehicle
Restroom:	Yes; barrier-free
Wheelchair/Stroller Access:	Limited to visitor center portions of loop trail
Drinking Water:	Yes; at visitor center. Water bottles suggested for hike
Picnic Area:	Yes
Lodging:	No
Camping:	Yes; open from late spring through early fall. Contact: Coconino National Forest, Peaks Ranger Station, 5010 N. Hwy 89, Flagstaff, AZ 86004, 928-526-0866
Suitable for:	All ages
Notes/Tips:	No gasoline or restaurants. Pets not allowed in visitor center or on trails. Lava rock is extremely sharp. Wear hiking boots or closed-toe shoes. Stay on the trail.

On a winter morning, A.D. 1064, a semi-active volcano erupted with a force equal to the explosive yield of a nuclear bomb. The blast leveled and incinerated all living things within a 7-mile radius. In the aftermath, all that was left was a 1,000-foot tall volcanic cone and an enormous lava field.

Sunset Crater Volcano National Monument serves as a stark reminder of the violent geological past that shaped north-central Arizona. The visitor center features an educational film, exhibits and a seismograph station. A 1-mile self-guiding loop trail at the base of the volcano allows visitors to examine the volcanic features and barren, but very impressive volcanic field. The Sunset Crater cinder cone is closed to hikers and climbers. Other nearby volcanoes can be explored. Ask for details at the visitor center.

Sunset Crater Volcano National Monument, 2717 N. Steves Blvd., Suite 3, Flagstaff, AZ 86004, 928-556-7042

21 Grand Falls

Location:	Off IR 6910 on the Navajo Indian Reservation
Best Time to Visit:	March, April
Visitor Center/Museum:	No
Hours:	N/A
Fee Area:	No
Restroom:	No
Wheelchair/Stroller Access:	No
Picnic Area:	Yes
Lodging:	No
Camping:	Yes; but you must bring all supplies
Suitable for:	All ages
Notes/Tips:	Although not difficult to find, a good map is needed. Locate Winona just east of Flagstaff on I-40, and go from there. Although IR 70 also goes to Grand Falls, and the distance is four miles less than IR 6910. Your vehicle, and your backside, will thank you. Unless the road is wet, the drive is suitable for passenger cars. Keep a close eye on kids when gazing at the falls. Watch for rattlesnakes.

Often called the Niagara Falls of Arizona, Grand Falls on the Little Colorado River is a part-time waterfall. In a winter when there has been decent snowfall in the mountains, the spring runoff transforms the normally tame Little Colorado into a raging torrent. On a windy plateau on the Navajo Reservation, the Little Colorado pours over a double cliff wall before continuing the journey west to join with the big Colorado.

Grand Falls is about 200 feet high, and almost 400 feet across. The muddy water roaring over the cliff is a truly visual treat and deafening experience. This is one natural wonder that all Arizonan's should see.

Grand Falls on the Little Colorado River, On IR 6910 on the Navajo Reservation

Wupatki
22 National Monument

Location:	22 miles north of Sunset Crater Visitor Center on the Sunset Loop Rd. Map available at Sunset Crater Visitor Center
Best Time to Visit:	Spring, fall, early winter
Visitor Center/Museum:	Yes; educational & entertaining
Hours:	Daily 8 a.m.-5 p.m.; closed Christmas
Fee Area:	Yes; $4 per vehicle
Restroom:	Yes; barrier-free
Wheelchair/Stroller Access:	Yes; a few of the walking trails may require extra help
Drinking Water:	Yes; but bring a water bottle
Picnic Area:	Yes
Lodging:	No
Camping:	See Sunset Crater
Suitable for:	All ages
Notes/Tips:	On the road between Sunset Crater & Wupatki, stop at the Painted Desert Vista for spectacular views of the Colorado Plateau & Painted Desert. Summers are hot, and in winter blizzards & freezing temperatures are common.

Twenty-two miles beyond Sunset Crater, you'll discover one of the most astounding national monuments in the country. Wupatki National Monument occupies 56 square-miles of dry, rugged land on the southwestern Colorado Plateau, containing some of Arizona's most remarkable ruins.

Begin your exploration at the visitor center, adjacent to Wupatki Pueblo, the largest ruin within monument boundaries. A short self-guided walking trail leads to the main ruin complex, the ancient ball court (which you can enter) and a strange "blow hole" that connects to a series of deep, subterranean caves. With changes in barometric pressure, air is either drawn in or forced out of the surface vent. Kids will delight in experiencing this natural phenomena.

Other ruins within the monument are also accessible by trail. I suggest spending about an hour at Wupatki and the rest of a morning or afternoon visiting nearby Lomaki, Citadel, Nalakihu and Wukoki Ruins. All of the accessible ruins are, at the most, a half-mile walk from pullouts off paved roads. Maps are available at the visitor center.

This is a must see on your journey through north-central Arizona.

Wupatki National Monument, HC 33, Box 444A, Flagstaff, AZ 86004, (928) 556-7040

◆ ──────────────── ◆

Little Colorado River Gorge

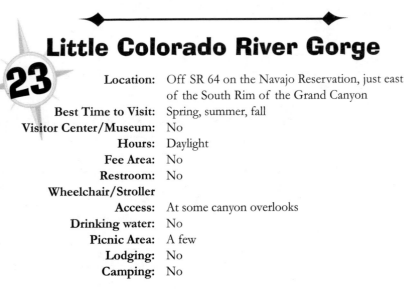

Location:	Off SR 64 on the Navajo Reservation, just east of the South Rim of the Grand Canyon
Best Time to Visit:	Spring, summer, fall
Visitor Center/Museum:	No
Hours:	Daylight
Fee Area:	No
Restroom:	No
Wheelchair/Stroller Access:	At some canyon overlooks
Drinking water:	No
Picnic Area:	A few
Lodging:	No
Camping:	No

Suitable for: All ages
Notes/Tips: Keep a close eye on kids near the canyon drop offs

The mighty Colorado River carved a giant gash in the earth. The Little Colorado River also did a number on the plateau near the Grand Canyon. The Little Colorado River Gorge is a deep, very narrow fissure that is just as breathtaking, although on a smaller scale, as the Grand Canyon. From several overlooks just off the highway, you can gaze upon this natural wonder and take photographs to your heart's delight. You might also want to do a little shopping at one of the many roadside stands where Navajo artisans and vendors sell everything from magnificent jewelry to Navajo tacos and Indian fry bread.

Little Colorado River Gorge, On SR 64 near the Grand Canyon's South Rim

Grand Canyon Railway

24

Location:	Williams is 30 miles west of Flagstaff on I-40; the train departs from the Williams Depot located on Grand Canyon Blvd. in Williams
Best Time to Visit:	Anytime
Visitor Center/Museum:	Yes; before boarding, check-out this remarkable museum
Hours:	Departs daily except Dec. 24-25
Fee Area:	Yes; seasonal and varied; call ahead for details
Restrooms:	Yes
Wheelchair/Stroller Access:	Yes; both at the depot & on the train. Train is equipped with chair lifts. Aisles & restrooms are accessible
Drinking Water:	Yes
Picnic Area:	Yes
Lodging:	Yes
Camping:	No
Suitable for:	All ages
Notes/Tips:	Rates, schedules & accommodation availability are subject to change. Make plans & reservations well in advance. Non-smoking train

If you're planning on visiting Arizona's most famous attraction, step aboard the Grand Canyon Railway for a trip that you'll never forget.

Even if you've visited the Grand Canyon on several occasions, riding the rails across 65 miles of beautiful countryside including pine forests, high desert plains and small canyons is both exciting and relaxing.

The Grand Canyon train departs at 9 a.m. from the small mountain community of Williams and arrives at Grand Canyon Village before noon. You have more than three hours to walk the rim trails or enjoy a narrated motorcoach tour. The train returns to Williams at 5:30 p.m. On the return trip, kids will enjoy the train robbery staged by horseback riding bandits.

Passengers can choose from three classes of service in authentically-restored Harriman train cars. A number of packages and options, including lodging at the historic Fray Marcos Hotel in Williams, are offered. Reservations are recommended.

Grand Canyon Railway Business Office, 123 N. San Francisco, Suite 210, Flagstaff, AZ 86001, 800-843-8724, FAX: 928-773-1976

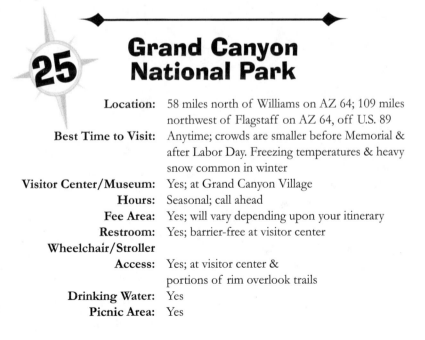

Grand Canyon National Park

25

Location:	58 miles north of Williams on AZ 64; 109 miles northwest of Flagstaff on AZ 64, off U.S. 89
Best Time to Visit:	Anytime; crowds are smaller before Memorial & after Labor Day. Freezing temperatures & heavy snow common in winter
Visitor Center/Museum:	Yes; at Grand Canyon Village
Hours:	Seasonal; call ahead
Fee Area:	Yes; will vary depending upon your itinerary
Restroom:	Yes; barrier-free at visitor center
Wheelchair/Stroller Access:	Yes; at visitor center & portions of rim overlook trails
Drinking Water:	Yes
Picnic Area:	Yes

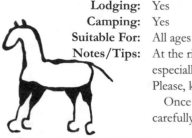

Lodging:	Yes
Camping:	Yes
Suitable For:	All ages
Notes/Tips:	At the rim overlooks, use extreme caution, especially with kids. Every year people fall. Please, keep a tight grip on your children.
	Once again, for a more rewarding experience, carefully plan your visit.

One mile deep, 190 miles long, and covering 1,900 square-miles, the Grand Canyon is Arizona's most famous natural attraction and one of the seven wonders of the world.

Discovered by Don Lopez de Cardenas, a captain in Coronado's expedition, Congress created Grand Canyon National Park in 1919.

Besides offering breathtaking scenery, whitewater rafting, superb hiking and camping, the park is also a haven for wildlife. You'll find 70 species of mammals, 250 species of birds, 25 species of reptiles and five species of amphibians.

The South Rim is the most visited portion of the park. During the summer, thousands of vacationers converge on Grand Canyon Village. Far fewer people explore the magnificent North Rim.

An entire book (and hundreds have been written) could be devoted to all there is to see and do at the Grand Canyon. Before your visit, do some homework. Gather information from the sources listed below, and carefully plan your trip. Please, don't limit your Grand Canyon discovery to a few quick stops at rim overlooks. If at all possible, stay a few days and *do* the Canyon.

Grand Canyon National Park, P.O. Box 129, Grand Canyon, AZ 86023, 928-638-7888

Grand Canyon National Park Lodges, P.O. Box 699, Grand Canyon, AZ 86023, 928-638-2401

Grand Canyon Chamber of Commerce, P.O. Box 3007, Grand Canyon, AZ 86023, 928-638-2807

For guided Canyon adventures, contact:

Grand Canyon Field Institute, P.O. Box 399, Grand Canyon, AZ 86023, 928-638-2485, FAX 928-638-2484, www.thecanyon.com/fieldinstitute

Grand Canyon Caverns

26

Location:	Off Historic Route 66, 22 miles west of Seligman
Best Time to Visit:	Spring, summer, fall
Visitor Center/Museum:	Yes; including gift shop and restaurant
Hours:	Daily; Summer: 8 a.m.-6 p.m.; Winter: 10 a.m.-5 p.m.; closed Christmas
Fee Area:	Yes; adults $9.50; ages 4-12 $6.75; under age 4 free
Restrooms:	Yes; barrier free
Wheelchair/Stroller Access:	Limited to visitor center, restaurant, and motel
Drinking Water:	Yes
Picnic Area:	Yes
Lodging:	Yes; at the adjacent Caverns Inn
Camping:	No
Suitable for:	All ages
Notes/Tips:	As with any underground experience, exploring a cave may be frightening for very young children. You know best.

Formed during the Mississippian Geologic Period, Grand Canyon Caverns is a natural wonder with a quirky history. About 200 feet beneath the earth, you'll discover a replica of a giant sloth that perished thousands of years ago (you can still see the claw marks on the cave wall where the huge animal tried in vain to climb out after falling into the cave), and wonder at what might have been if the former Soviet Union and the United States had started launching nuclear missiles.

On a 45-minute, 3/4 mile easy guided hike through the cave, you will spot ancient geological formations and fossilized animals. This cavern was also selected by the U.S. government as a natural bomb shelter. During the height of the Cold War, thousands of pounds of food, water, and survival supplies were stored in the cavern. They're still waiting for a nuclear holocaust that never happened. It's a chilling reminder of a frightening era.

Grand Canyon Caverns, P. O. Box 180, Peach Springs, AZ 86434, 928-422-3223

27 Paria River Canyon

Location:	At Lee's Ferry on the Colorado River
Best Time to Visit:	Late spring, early fall
Visitor Center/Museum:	No
Hours:	Daylight
Fee Area:	Hiking, wilderness fees may apply; call for details
Restrooms:	Yes; at Lee's Ferry
Wheelchair/Stroller Access:	No
Drinking Water:	Yes; see Notes/Tips
Picnic Area:	Yes
Lodging:	Yes
Camping:	Yes
Suitable for:	Best for experienced hikers
Notes/Tips:	Exploring Arizona's "slot" canyons can be potentially dangerous. Bring plenty of water, and proper hiking gear. I would strongly suggest consulting with an expert at a local hiking store prior to planning a trip. Always contact the Kanab BLM Field Office. Play particular attention to weather conditions. **Do not enter any "slot" canyons if there is even a remote possibility of rain. That decision could be fatal.** Ask the folks at the BLM about hiring a guide for this experience.

The bizarre, often photographed slot canyons on the Arizona/ Utah border are stunning testaments to the power of nature. These narrow, deep scars in the earth provide the careful explorer with the opportunity to take unique photographs of these mini-canyons that not many people visit. In fact, Arizona Highways magazine sponsors photography trips to the slot canyons. This might be your best bet for visiting this exciting region of Arizona. Just remember to plan carefully, and use your best good judgment when exploring these beautiful canyons.

Paria River Canyon, Kanab BLM Field Office, UT, 435-688-3200, http://paria.az.blm.gov/

Arizona's Newest National Monuments

━━━◆━━━━━━━━━━━━━━━━◆━━━

Just prior to leaving office, President Clinton signed Executive Orders creating five new national monuments in Arizona. They are: Grand Canyon-Parashant, Vermilion Cliffs, Agua Fria, Sonoran Desert, and Ironwood Forest.

As of this printing, all of these wilderness areas are very remote with only limited services. Visiting these monuments requires doing some homework. I would first contact the Sierra Club at www.arizona.sierraclub.org/monuments/. Just remember, these are rugged areas requiring careful planning before exploring. You might also visit an outdoor/hiking store near you for more information.

Ironwood Forest National Monument:

This 129,000-acre preserve encompasses the Silver Bell, Ragged Top, and Sawtooth Mountains. It contains one of the richest stands of ironwood trees in the Sonoran Desert. There are also over 200 sites from the Hohokam period. Ironwood Forest is located in extreme southeast Arizona.

Sonoran Desert National Monument:

This fascinating monument located in southwest Arizona contains an abundance of cultural resources, including evidence of ancient villages, campsites, rock art, and artifacts fo the prehistoric Hohokam and other native peoples. In addition, there are trails that extend back in time hundreds or even thousands of years used by local people to collect shells from the Sea of Cortez.

Grand Canyon-Parshant National Monument:

Bordering Grand Canyon National Park, this monument includes over one million acres of public land. Along with deep canyons, the boundaries alsos include portions of the Shivwits Plateau. This is prime habitat for bighorn sheep, various raptors and migratory birds, and pronghorn sheep.

Vermilion Cliffs National Monument:

Located in northern Arizona on 293,000 acres, this monument includes the Paria Canyon-Vermilion Cliffs Wilderness. In this rugged area, species of desert bighorn and pronghorn thrive. The monument also is the home to at least twenty species of raptors, including the California Condors, which have been reintroduced into the region.

Agua Fria National Monument:

Located only about 40 miles north of Phoenix, this monument includes both Perry Mesa and Black Mesa. In this 71,000-acre world of secret canyons, are found some of the most significant ancient ruins in the southwest—at least 450 prehistoric sites. This semi-desert area also includes some lush riparian habitat along the Agua Fria River and its tributaries.

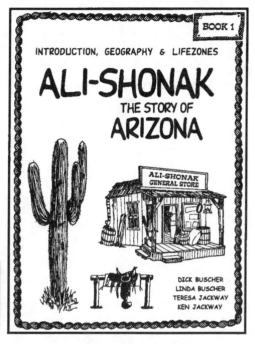